Contents

Condi
in the

Study co
of the Eu

Council of Europe Publishing, 2000 (2nd edition)

French edition:
Les conditions d'emploi dans la Charte sociale européenne
ISBN 92-871-4489-3

Council of Europe Publishing
F-67075 Strasbourg Cedex

ISBN 92-871-4490-7
© Council of Europe, November 2000 (2nd edition)
Printed in Germany

Part three – Fair remuneration

The European Social Charter – an overview

Counterpart to the European Convention on Human Rights which guarantees civil and political rights, the European Social Charter is a binding instrument setting out a broad range of economic and social rights.

Opened for signature on 18 October 1961 and entered into force on 26 February 1965, the Social Charter guarantees a series of rights organised in nineteen articles, to which the Additional Protocol of 5 May 1988 (entered into force on 4 September 1992) adds four further articles. The revised European Social Charter, opened for signature on 3 May 1996 and entered into force on 1 July 1999, revises and increases the number of rights guaranteed.[1]

Compliance with the undertakings provided in the Charter and the revised Charter is assessed by an international supervisory mechanism on the basis of reports[2] submitted every two years on the hard core provisions and every four years on the non-hard core provisions, by states having ratified either treaty.[3]

The supervision procedure functions as follows:

– *the European Committee of Social Rights*, composed of nine independent experts elected by the Committee of Ministers and assisted by an observer from the International Labour

---

[1]   The revised Social Charter brings together in a single instrument the rights contained in the Charter as amended, the rights contained in the Additional Protocol and a series of new rights organised in eight new articles.

[2]   These reports are public and may be consulted on the Internet (http:/www.humanrights.coe.int).

[3]   As of 1 November 2000, the Contracting Parties to the Social Charter are: Austria, Belgium, the Czech Republic, Denmark, Finland, Germany, Greece, Hungary, Iceland, Ireland, Luxembourg, Malta, the Netherlands, Norway, Poland, Portugal, Slovakia, Spain, Turkey and the United Kingdom. The Parties to the revised Charter are: Bulgaria, Cyprus, Estonia, France, Italy, Romania, Slovenia and Sweden.

Organisation, examines the reports submitted by states and makes an observation on whether the Charter is being respected by the states. These assessments are called "conclusions".

– *the Committee of Ministers of the Council of Europe* follows through the Conclusions of the European Committee of Social Rights. It may issue a recommendation to a state, requiring it to amend its legislation or practice in order to put the situation in conformity with the Charter. It is supported in this task by *the Governmental Committee*, composed of representatives of states having ratified the Charter and assisted by observers representing the international social partners. This Committee elaborates the decisions of the Committee of Ministers, i.e. it selects from cases of non-conformity with the Charter those situations which should be the subject of recommendations. This selection is made on the basis of social, economic and other policy considerations.

The Additional Protocol providing for a system of collective complaints was opened for signature on 9 November 1995 and entered into force on 1 July 1998.[1] This Protocol adds to the system of examining government reports a collective complaints procedure to deal with alleged breaches of the Charter, thus improving the effectiveness of the Charter's supervisory machinery.

Who may submit a collective complaint?

– European employers' organisations and European trade unions which participate in the work of the Governmental Committee, i.e. the European Trade Union Confederation (ETUC), the Union of the Confederations of Industry and Employers of Europe (UNICE) and the International Organisation of Employers (IOE);

---

[1]   As of 1 November 2000, ten states have accepted the collective complaints procedure: Bulgaria, Cyprus, Finland, France, Greece, Italy, Norway, Portugal, Slovenia and Sweden.

— European non-governmental organisations with consultative status with the Council of Europe[1] included on a list drawn up for this purpose by the Governmental Committee (approximately fifty organisations);[2]

— national organisations of employers and trade unions from the state concerned.

In addition, each state may, in a declaration to the Secretary General of the Council of Europe, authorise national non-governmental organisations to lodge complaints against it. To date, Finland has made such a declaration.

In what form?

There is no standard form for lodging collective complaints. They must be in writing and signed by an authorised representative of the complainant organisation.

In which language?

The official languages of the Council of Europe are English and French.

Complaints lodged by the European Trade Union Confederation (ETUC), the Union of the Confederations of Industry and Employers of Europe (UNICE) and the International Organisation of Employers (IOE) or by international non-governmental organisations included in a list established for this purpose must be written in English or French.

---

[1]   For more information on the procedure for attaining consultative status at the Council of Europe consult NGO-Unit@coe.int.

[2]   Interested organisations should send a letter to the Secretariat of the European Social Charter: Directorate General of Human Rights – DG II, Council of Europe, F-67075 Strasbourg Cedex (France). The letter should be accompanied by detailed documentation including in particular the status of the organisation; its field of activity and its objectives and methods of working. This dossier will be forwarded to the Governmental Committee for a decision.

Complaints lodged by national employers' or trade union organisations or by national non-governmental organisations from the Contracting Party concerned may be submitted in a non-official language.

What should the complaint contain?

The complaint must contain the following information:

— the name and contact details of the organisation lodging the complaint;

— in the case of non-governmental organisations, a mention that the organisation has consultative status with the Council of Europe and is included in the Governmental Committee list, and details of the fields in which it is active;

— the name of the state against which the complaint is being lodged (the state in question must have accepted the collective complaints procedure);

— the Charter provisions concerned by the complaint (all of which must have been accepted by the state in question);

— an indication as to what extent the state in question is alleged not to have ensured satisfactory application of certain Charter provisions, supported by relevant arguments;

— copies of relevant documentation.

How does the European Committee of Social Rights examine the complaint?

The complaint is examined by the European Committee of Social Rights, which first decides on their admissibility in the light of the criteria listed in the Protocol and of its rules of procedure.

If the complaint is admissible, a written procedure takes place with an exchange of documents between the parties and, in certain cases, consultation with European social partners. The procedure may become an oral one and a hearing may be organised by the Committee.

The Committee then decides on the merits of the complaint. Its decision is contained in a report that is transmitted to the Committee of Ministers.

Finally, the Committee of Ministers adopts a resolution closing the procedure. In the event that the European Committee of Social Rights finds a breach of the Charter, the Committee may address a recommendation to the state concerned, requesting it to amend its legislation or practice in order to comply with the Charter.

Introduction

The first theme that appears in the European Social Charter is employment. The right to work is set out in Article 1, followed by various rights concerning working conditions laid down in Articles 2, 3 and 4. The logic of this sequence is clear: the commitment to high levels of employment in Article 1 is accompanied by an obligation to secure a satisfactory level of protection for workers in relation to working time, health and safety at work, and fair remuneration. These guarantees are at the very heart of the employment model in Europe, despite the considerable pressure brought to bear by political, economic and demographic developments across the continent and throughout the world. All states party to the Charter have had to face new challenges in the labour market in their quest for high quality, durable employment, in particular the call for less employment regulation and lower labour charges. These challenges have been equally felt by management and labour, who have the task of negotiating more flexible labour arrangements, especially in the area of working time and overtime.

Although the Charter was drafted in the context of very different economic conditions, the rights that it guarantees are as necessary now as ever before. In the field of health and safety, the European Committee of Social Rights has kept abreast of huge technological changes in the work place which have reduced risks in some areas, but also given rise to new hazards. The Committee has turned to more recent international instruments which address hazards in the work place in order to elucidate the obligations under Article 3 of the Charter, such as the series of European Union directives on health and safety at work, the standards of the International Labour Organisation and the International Commission on Radiological Protection. Constant vigilance is called for on the part of the Committee, as well as national authorities, to verify whether workers are adequately protected against new risks. Reflecting the extent of part-time or temporary working in many sectors of the economy, the Committee has shown particular concern in ensuring that these workers benefit in full from measures to protect their health and safety at work.

The right to a fair remuneration is a key element of social justice. The Charter is unique in setting down a European standard on the issue of adequate remuneration. The difficulties inherent in adjudicating compliance with this right have been considerable over the years, and further challenges lie ahead with the increasing number of ratifications of the Charter. Nevertheless, as this publication shows, it is possible to assess wage levels across Europe using the criterion of fairness. The recent moves towards a statutory minimum wage in a number of Contracting Parties attest to the widely-held concern that employment should be fairly rewarded.

The aim of this publication is to present an overview of the case law built up over the years by the European Committee of Social Rights in the fields covered by Articles 2, 3 and 4 of the European Social Charter. It includes the Committee's most recent assessments of compliance with these provisions, published in December 1998 (Conclusions XIV-2).

Part one – Working hours

1.   Article 2 of the Charter secures the right to just conditions of work. Its main focus is on various aspects of working time – daily, weekly, annual holidays. The Committee emphasises that in guaranteeing just conditions of work, the Charter protects the health and safety of workers, as well as their private and family lives.

2.   All paragraphs in this article are subject to the application of Article 33 of the Charter. Therefore, states may be considered to be in compliance with their obligations if they can demonstrate that the rights concerned are secured for the "great majority" of workers through collective agreements or other means. For the purpose of the Charter, the phrase "great majority" is interpreted as meaning 80 % of the workforce. This means that a significant proportion of the workforce (up to 20 %) may be excluded from the benefit of these rights without the Charter being violated. Early on, the Committee expressed its regret at this arrangement,[1] but must apply the clear text of the Charter. This is not always a straightforward task.

3.   In order to consider the effect of Article 33 on assessment of state compliance, the Committee first reviews the relevant legal framework. For example, where it detects non-conformity with the Charter in a legal measure of general application, it is unnecessary to try to establish the number of workers actually affected, since all workers may be concerned. A good example of this is the case of Belgium's non-compliance with Article 2 para. 1. In one regard, the situation was deemed to be in breach of the Charter since the working time flexibility schemes permitted by law fail to provide the necessary guarantees (see below) and all workers could be concerned.[2] Article 33 was relevant however in assessing whether the

---

[1] Conclusions IV, p. xv.

[2] See also the conclusions for the Netherlands and Norway in cycle XIV-2.

categories excluded from the main statute (Act of 16 March 1971 on working time) exceeded 20% of the labour force. The Committee found that they did not. In other cases, where the Committee has not been in possession of sufficient labour market data, it has had to defer its assessment until the national authorities provide sufficient statistical evidence[1].

4.   The five paragraphs of Article 2 which also appear in Article 2 of the revised Charter remain subject to the "80% rule" (Article I para. 2).

I.   Reasonable working hours

5.   Under Article 2 para. 1 states undertake "to provide for reasonable daily and weekly working hours, the working week to be progressively reduced to the extent that the increase in productivity and other relevant factors permit".

6.   The aim of this provision is to protect the health and safety of workers, since accidents at work are more likely to happen where workers are occupied for long hours over a considerable period of time[2]. This provision also seeks to secure respect for the private and family life of the worker, since working time should neither be too long nor so variable as to unduly disrupt the rest of the worker's time. Clearly, other interests are at stake, especially economic. Therefore, in supervising compliance with this provision, the Committee's task is to examine all relevant factors, state by state, and decide whether the rules and/or practice in the area of working time are reasonable within the meaning of the Charter. While there is thus no precise, abstract definition of reasonableness, the Committee has nonetheless indicated that excessively long working time (16 hours per day, 60 hours per week) will be a violation of the Charter in any circumstances.

7.   In order to comply with this provision, Contracting Parties must demonstrate that daily and weekly working time is subject to reasonable limits imposed by statute, regulation, collective agree-

---

[1] See for example Conclusions XIV-2, Luxembourg, p.465.

[2] Cf. Conclusions XIV-2, p.32, also Iceland, pp. 364-365.

ment or any other obligatory means involving supervision by an appropriate authority[1]. The relevant national rules must encompass both normal working time and overtime, as it is the total length of working time which must be reasonable.

8.   Information on working time is not always readily available, but is essential in the supervision of this provision. Data on average working time is not sufficient, since this will not reveal the longest working days and weeks. Where the matter is largely regulated by collective agreement, as contemplated in Article 33, comprehensive information on the contents of such agreements must be provided to the Committee. National reports should refer to the principal labour market sectors and indicate the working time rules that apply to the great majority of workers.

9.   The question of labour inspection in the area of working time is significant. One of the general obligations imposed by the Charter is to maintain a system of labour inspection appropriate to national conditions (Article 20 para. 5). The Committee therefore frequently seeks information on the activity of labour inspection authorities at national level, this being a valuable gauge of the level of compliance in practice with national and Charter standards in this area.

10.   The text of the Charter also envisages reductions in working time to the extent that productivity and other factors permit. Among these other factors are the nature of the work, including any particular risks posed to workers' health and safety. Perusal of recent conclusions reveals that in most states, standard working time is decreasing. Similarly, increased restrictions have been placed on overtime working in certain states, for example, a limit of eighty hours' overtime per year in Spain[2].

11.   The emergence of new working time regimes in recent years has challenged traditional notions of standard daily and weekly time, and overtime. The adoption within the European Union of the Working Time Directive[3], and its subsequent entry into force

---

[1] Conclusions I, p. 169.

[2] Conclusions XIV-2, p. 668.

[3] Council Directive 93/104/EC of 23 November 1993 concerning certain aspects of the organisation of working time, OJ No. L 307/18, 13.12.93.

created a new legal framework in this area for many of the states which are bound by Article 2 para. 1 of the Charter. Therefore, in its most recent assessment of compliance with this provision, the Committee paid close attention to national situations that were significantly altered through the implementation of the 1993 Directive. While declaring that flexible working arrangements are not in principle contrary to the Charter, the Committee underlines that the precise features of the various national schemes must abide by the standards of the Charter. States must provide full details on, *inter alia*, the relevant legal framework, the various arrangements that are permitted, the scope for derogation on the basis of collective agreement, and the maximum daily and weekly hours that must still be respected. This matter is considered in greater detail below.

A.   Daily working time

12.   As mentioned above, the Committee considers that where it is permissible for a worker to work for more than sixteen hours per day, or sixty hours in any week, the situation will be deemed contrary to the Charter (subject to the application of Article 33). On this basis, the Committee concluded that Norway is in violation of the Charter since the Working Environment Act permits exceptions to the standard duration of daily and weekly work (nine hours per day and forty hours per week). Section 49 of the act allows, in certain circumstances, for longer overtime working. This may be done by collective agreement and reach as long as sixteen hours per twenty-four hour period. The Committee considered that since Section 49 was rather generally phrased, and was not limited to any section of the economy, Article 33 could not be relied on to alter its negative assessment. It underlined that even if weekly limits remained in conformity with the Charter, this could not compensate for the unduly long working day that the law permits. Other safeguards were cited, such as the need for the worker's consent, the limitation of any such agreement to three months and the restriction of such arrangements to companies bound by collective agreements, but the Committee took the view that none

of these considerations could vary its negative assessment of the situation[1].

13. Excessively long working days were found to be permitted in Finland, where national law (the Working Hours Act of 1996) allows for daily rest periods to be reduced temporarily from the standard eleven hours to seven hours or even, in stated circumstances, to five hours (for a maximum of three days). This situation was found to be in clear violation of Article 2 para. 1. The procedural safeguards surrounding the reduction of daily rest time to seven hours did not alter this assessment[2].

14. Iceland was found to violate the Charter on similar grounds. No maximum limit is prescribed for daily and weekly working time, apart from minimum rest periods. In certain cases, the daily rest period can be shortened to just eight hours, which allows for a working day that is not compatible with Article 2 para. 1[3].

B. *Weekly working time*

15. Other instances of violations of the Charter on the issue of working time result from insufficient statutory protection against excessive weekly working hours. The Committee found that Ireland failed to implement the Charter in this regard, since the legislation in force during the reference period under consideration omitted a considerable portion of the working population and, in any event, permitted a working week of up to sixty hours, or even longer in the hotel business[4].

16. The Committee found that Belgium was in violation of the Charter on the basis, *inter alia,* that under certain working time

---

[1] Conclusions XIV-2, pp. 576-578.

[2] *ibid.*, pp. 217-218.

[3] *ibid.*, 363-364.

[4] The legislation in question dates from 1936 and 1938. Subsequent to the reference period under examination in Cycle XIV-2, new legislation was introduced to implement the EU Working Time Directive. This legislation has yet to be examined by the Committee.

arrangements, no maximum weekly limit was stipulated[1]. Similarly, as regards Spain, the Committee found that the Workers' Statute permitted a working week of up to sixty hours or more, since the daily rest period of twelve hours would permit a working day of the same duration, and the weekly rest period may be carried over to the following week[2]. Other states have been question about daily and weekly maxima, where national reports have not indicated these with sufficient clarity[3].

17.   See Section D below on the closely related issue of weekly rest periods.

C.   Flexible working arrangements

18.   As mentioned above, the Committee gave in-depth consideration to the phenomenon of flexible working time in Conclusions XIV-2 and its consequences for the health and safety of workers, and their private and family lives. It identified a number of factors that guide its assessment of national situations:

1.   Unreasonably long daily and weekly hours must be guarded against

19.   The maximum limits identified by the Committee for daily and weekly work must not be exceeded. Since flexibility schemes offer many different alternatives, with scope for further variation at the level of the workplace, the Committee exercises particular vigilance in ensuring that the maximum limits permissible under Article 2 para. 1 are respected. The detailed assessments of the Finnish and Norwegian situations during cycle XIV-2 are good examples of the Committee's approach.

---

[1] Conclusions XIV-2, pp. 111-115.

[2] *ibid.*, pp. 668-669.

[3] For example, Finland and Greece in Conclusions XIV-2.

2. A precise legal framework

20. Flexible working time constitutes a significant departure from the traditional manner of regulation in this field. Nevertheless, it must still operate within a precise legal framework that clearly delimits the scope available to employers and workers to modify working time. The level at which social partners may agree is relevant, since the Charter requires extra safeguards where company level agreements are possible. In so ruling, the Committee has clarified that adequate procedural guarantees are an essential element in compliance with Article 2 para. 1.

21. The Committee's focus on this aspect of flexibility has led it to a negative assessment in a number of cases. In relation to Belgium, the Committee considered that the "Limited flexibility scheme" violated the Charter, although the maximum daily and weekly periods of work allowed were within the limits mentioned above. The Committee underlined that the possibility for employers to change work schedules in the absence of an agreement with staff representatives, as well as the alternative possibility of doing so on the basis of a company-level agreement, failed to offer sufficient safeguards to workers[1]. In the case of France, the Committee repeated its view, requesting regular information on collective agreements dealing with this subject[2].

22. The Netherlands was also found to be in breach of its obligation under this provision on the basis that a working week of up to sixty hours may be provided for in company-level agreements (under the so-called "flexibility regulations"). Where no there are no staff representatives or trade union delegates in the workforce, or where agreement is not reached, the employer may vary working time in a more limited manner (under the so-called "basic regulations"). Although the threshold of sixty hours was not exceeded, the situation was found to violate the Charter since long hours (up to sixty, or fifty-four, depending on the applicable regulations) could be agreed to or imposed without adequate procedural safeguards[3].

---

[1] *Ibid.*, pp. 113-114.

[2] *Ibid.*, p. 256.

[3] *Ibid.*, pp. 533-536.

This conclusion may be compared to that for Norway, mentioned above, where the safeguards in national law appeared more effective[1], but could not remedy a situation found to violate the Charter on other grounds.

3.   Reasonable averaging periods

23.   The averaging of working time over a reference period of several months has become widespread practice. For the purposes of Article 2 para. 1, a reference period of four to six months is acceptable. Longer periods (up to one year) may be considered to be in conformity with Article 2 para. 1 in exceptional circumstances[2].

24.   Other issues that the Committee has signalled it may investigate under this provision are the protection of part-time workers and the situation of workers "on call" or working discontinuous hours. The role of labour inspection, referred to above, will also figure in the assessment of state compliance with this provision.

D.   Weekly rest period

25.   Article 2 para. 5 of the Charter provides for "a weekly rest period which shall, as far as possible, coincide with the day recognised by tradition or custom in the country or region concerned as a day of rest".

26.   It is very clear from this text that two obligations are concerned: the first, expressed in absolute terms, is the obligation to provide for a period of rest each week. The second obligation, ensuring that this day coincides with the traditional day of rest, is qualified by the words "as far as possible". In all of the Contracting States, the traditional day of rest is Sunday. States do not enjoy total discretion in allotting weekly rest periods, however. The Committee has taken care to restate that the weekly rest may fall on another day, but only where the nature of the work so requires

---

[1] Especially the requirement to obtain the worker's consent.

[2] *Ibid.*, p. 34.

(health service, tourist industry, continuous shift work, transport) or on account of the characteristics of the economy[1]. It takes note of national situations where an unusually high number of workers work on Sunday, either regularly or occasionally, eg. 36% in Ireland, 40% in the United Kingdom[2].

27. While it may be possible for a worker to work on the traditional weekly rest day, it is prohibited to deny them an alternative day of rest. National law must forbid any waiver of the right to a weekly rest period, even in return for a higher rate of pay[3]. Nevertheless, in examining recent legislative changes in states in response to the European Union Working Time Directive, the Committee takes the view that postponing the weekly rest period to the following week does not automatically breach the Charter. However, the worker must be able to work on no more than twelve consecutive days, followed by two rest days[4]. In this way, the intention behind this provision – safeguarding the health and safety of the worker as well as protecting their private and family life – is still achieved.

28. The Committee's concern to ensure that sufficient safe-guards are retained where the issue of working time is subject to collective bargaining is also evident in relation Article 2 para. 5. In the case of France, for example, it observed that where exceptions to weekly rest periods may be made through company-level collective agreements, the level of protection of workers is low-ered[5].

---

[1] Conclusions XIV-2, Luxembourg, p. 468.

[2] These figures were quoted in cycle XIV-2.

[3] Conclusions XIV-2, pp. 34-35.

[4] This means that the Working Time Directive is not incompatible with the Charter on this issue, since it provides for a weekly rest period of thirty-five hours (Article 5), using a reference period of two weeks (Article 16).

[5] Conclusions XIV-2, p. 259.

II. The right to holidays

29. The right of workers to holidays pursues the same goal as the right to reasonable working time, seeking to ensure the health and safety of workers and to protect their private and family lives. Since this is an essential issue for workers, the Committee is vigilant against any tendency to diminish these rights, in particular arrangements that permit workers to forego their holiday entitlements for extra pay.

A. Public holidays with pay

30. Under Article 2 para. 2, states undertake "to provide for public holidays with pay".

31. The first thing to note about this guarantee is that although states must ensure that workers benefit from public holidays with pay, the Charter does not specify a minimum number of such days. This may both reflect and partly explain the wide variation observed through the years from state to state in the matter of public holidays, ranging from just six to as many as seventeen[1]. More recently, states seem to grant between ten and twelve public holidays per year.

32. Similar variation may be observed in the legal basis for public holidays, which may be legislation, collective agreement or custom, especially in the case of religious feast days[2]. There may also be regional differences within countries. This does not pose a problem of compliance with the Charter, which merely insists that workers must benefit from some paid public holidays. States need to demonstrate that wages are not reduced on account of a public holiday.

33. If some workers are obliged to work on a public holiday because of the particular nature of their employment, they should

---

[1] United Kingdom and Italy respectively, in the first supervision cycle.

[2] For example, Conclusions XIV-2, Netherlands, p. 536.

be granted compensatory leave. The Committee has stressed that the very purpose of the provision would be defeated if such work did not attract compensatory leave[1]. Also, work on public holidays should not be commonplace. The Committee raises this issue with states as part of its assessment. It expressed the view in Cycle XIV-2 that Portuguese law on this point was rather non-specific and sought further information on the situation in practice.

34.   However, the Committee has found the situation in Finland to be in conformity with the Charter even though work performed on certain public holidays may give rise to payment in lieu of compensatory leave at a later date, if the worker so desires[2]. It considered that the general principle that compensatory leave is required by the Charter in such circumstances could admit of certain well-defined exceptions with the worker's consent. In Finland, no person can be required to work on every public holiday, the circumstances in which this is possible are clearly stated in law, and the worker is entitled to a higher rate of pay. These factors were sufficient to ensure that the required level of protection was maintained. In contrast, the Committee found that Portugal was in breach of this provision on the basis that, in firms employing more than ten persons, work performed on a public holiday attracts a compensatory rest period of just 25% of the time worked. Since this rule may affect a considerable proportion of the working population, Article 33 did not apply[3].

35.   In certain states, when a public holiday coincides with the weekend, the day off is awarded on another date. While this practice is noted, it is not an essential element in compliance with the Charter[4].

---

[1] Conclusions XIII-1, Greece, p. 73.

[2] Conclusions XIV-2, p. 220.

[3] *Ibid.*, pp. 630-631.

[4] For example, Conclusions XIII-2, Belgium, p. 241.

B.   *Annual leave entitlement*

36.   Under Article 2 para. 3, states undertake "to provide for a minimum of two weeks' annual holiday with pay".

37.   Given the advances made in this field since the adoption of the Charter, and especially the adoption within the European Union of the Working Time Directive, there are few problems in the implementation of this provision. Annual holiday entitlement in Europe typically ranges from four to six weeks or even longer. Nevertheless, the principles that flow from the case law of the Committee require more careful scrutiny of national situations. Above all, states must establish the necessary framework to ensure the effective application of this right[1].

38.   It was established in the first supervision cycle that the Charter does not permit the waiver of annual leave in return for pay, even with the freely-given consent of the worker[2]. On this basis, Malta has been found not to comply with the Charter[3]. However, it is permissible for workers to receive payment in lieu of unused leave at the expiration of the employment contract.

39.   Although two weeks' leave is short by contemporary stan-dards, the Committee remains vigilant against any arrangements that could have the effect of depriving workers of even this entitle-ment. One example is where the worker's leave entitlement may be deferred until later in the year, or until the following year. Sea-sonal workers in Finland may find themselves in such a situation, prompting the Committee to recall that the Charter requires at least two weeks' leave in each year. Further information on the situation practice is awaited[4]. In a similar vein, the Committee has consid-

---

[1] Conclusions XIV-2, United Kingdom, p. 759.

[2] Conclusions I, p. 170.

[3] Conclusions XIV-2, p. 503. In contrast, the possibility in Finland of providing payment in lieu of holidays to part-time workers who work between six hours and fourteen days per month was not deemed to violate the Charter on account of the application of Article 33 – *ibid.*, p.222.

[4] *Ibid.*, p. 221.

ered the impact of accident or illness occurring during the worker's annual leave. Where this arises, the Charter requires that the worker be entitled to take the leave days "lost" to illness or accident at another time, so that they benefit from the obligatory minimum period of two weeks per year[1]. State practice in this regard is systematically checked[2]. Two particular restrictions have been considered recently. In Germany, a worker who loses holidays through illness is entitled to defer their leave entitlement, but only until the end of the same year, or, in the case of transfer, until the end of the first trimester of the following year. While certain exceptions are permitted, the Committee has enquired whether the effect of this rule could be to deny workers a minimum leave period of two weeks in each year[3]. A different scenario exists in Norway, where a worker is not entitled to defer holiday entitlement until the sixth day of illness. The Committee considered that this rule is not incompatible with the Charter since workers normally receive twenty-five days' leave per year and would, therefore, still enjoy more than the minimum stipulated by the Charter[4].

40.   Like all Charter provisions, Article 2 paragraph 3 is subject to Article 31, paragraph 1 of which allows for such restrictions or limitations "as are prescribed by law and are necessary in a democratic society for the protection of the rights and freedom of others or for the protection of public interest, national security, public health or morals". The Committee has had occasion to consider restrictions of this nature in relation to Cyprus, where national law empowers the Minister of Labour and Social Security to issue an order postponing the taking of leave if the public interest so requires. Referring to the interpretation of the phrase "public interest" by national courts, the Committee considered that the situation was not incompatible with the Charter. Noting that the

---

[1] Conclusions XII-2, p. 62.

[2] During supervision cycle XIV-2 further details were sought on this point from Denmark, Germany, Greece, Iceland, Italy, Malta and the United Kingdom.

[3] Conclusions XIV-2, p. 295.

[4] *Ibid.*, p. 580.

power had never been used, it requested to be informed of any recourse to it in future[1].

41.   Subjecting the right to annual leave to a qualifying period of up to twelve months, as in Sweden, has been found not to violate the Charter[2]. Similarly, the reduction of annual leave in proportion to length of service during the first year of employment is not inconsistent with the Charter[3]. A similar restriction, which, although it granted the full quota of annual leave, reduced holiday pay proportionately where the worker had not served a full year, was considered not to infringe the Charter[4].

III.   Reducing working time in dangerous or unhealthy occupations

42.   In addition to the provisions described above, which are of general concern, the Charter also makes special provision for workers whose occupation may expose them to health risks. Under Article 2 para. 4, states undertake "to provide for additional paid holidays or reduced working hours for workers engaged in dangerous or unhealthy occupations as prescribed". Article 33 applies to this provision, as to the other paragraphs of Article 2, but with the difference that here the reference to "the great majority of workers" only concerns workers engaged in hazardous occupations.

43.   This provision leaves a certain discretion to states, since the occupations at issue are those defined by the state itself as dangerous or unhealthy. Nevertheless, the Committee has stated that national regulations designating hazardous jobs are subject to review, so that any state failing to recognise manifest dangers in certain occupations could be in breach of its obligation[5]. Accordingly, the Committee regularly questions states about the occupa-

---

[1] *Ibid.*, p. 161.

[2] *Ibid.*, p. 702.

[3] Conclusions VII, Ireland, p. 14.

[4] Conclusions VI, Sweden, p. 13.

[5] Conclusions II, p. 9.

tions officially designated as hazardous, as well as activities which it considers to be clearly covered by this provision – steelworks, shipyards, metal processing, chemical and pharmaceutical activities, carpentry and building, exposure to ionising radiation, extremes of temperature, noise etc. [1] Technological developments over the years have lead to improved safety in many areas of industry, as well as increased awareness of harmful phenomena such as physical and mental stress and long-term exposure to certain materials and processes. As the Committee often states, Article 2 para. 4 remains an essential element in worker protection for as long as they may encounter risks to their health and safety in the course of their employment[2]. States must provide detailed information on the measures taken to implement this provision; otherwise the Committee cannot make its assessment of compliance[3].

44.   The obligation under this provision is to reduce working time or grant additional holidays to the workers concerned. The Charter does not specify the magnitude of the reduction or the number of extra holidays. It is not compatible with the Charter to permit increased pay to be offered instead[4]. The Netherlands Government has argued that the purpose of this provision is satisfied if the period of exposure, rather than overall working time is reduced. The Committee did not consider this sufficient, and called on the Dutch authorities to supplement their existing measures by providing for reduced working time or additional holidays as the only way of giving workers sufficient recovery time[5].

45.   A number of Contracting States have expressed the view in recent implementation reports that Article 2 para. 4 is somewhat unbalanced in its emphasis on reacting to hazardous working

---

[1] See for example the Conclusions for Austria, Germany and Norway during cycle XIV-2.

[2] See for example Conclusions XIV-2, Belgium, pp.117-118.

[3] See the Committee's comments to Austria, Spain and the United Kingdom under this provision during Cycle XIV-2.

[4] Addendum to Conclusions XIII-2, Luxembourg, p. 24.

[5] Conclusions XIV-2, p. 538.

conditions rather than seeking to eliminate or reduce risks[1]. It is significant that in the revised Charter, Article 2 para. 4 has been amended so as to concentrate on risk elimination and then, where risks are still present, working time should be reduced or additional holidays granted. The view of the Committee is that while an active and effective health and safety policy is essential (and already required by Article 3 para. 2), as long as risks remain in certain occupations, the obligation imposed by Article 2 para. 4 retains its relevance and urgency. Where workers are exposed to dangers or hazards in the course of their employment, shorter working hours or additional paid holidays help to reduce accumulation of physical and mental fatigue, risk exposure and permit the worker a longer period of rest. In several recent cases, the Committee has quoted high accident frequency in certain states as indicators that substantial risks to health and safety remain in a number of sectors, reinforcing the need for full compliance with Article 2 para. 4[2].

---

[1] See for example the conclusions for Belgium, Ireland and Italy during cycle XIV-2.

[2] *Ibid.*, Austria, p. 77; Portugal, pp. 632-633 and Spain, p. 670.

Part two – Health and safety at work

46.   Article 3 of the Social Charter requires Contracting Parties to guarantee the right to safe and healthy working conditions. The Committee regards this as *"a widely recognised principle, stemming directly from the right to personal integrity, one of the fundamental principles of human rights"*.[1] The purpose of Article 3 is thus directly related to that of Article 2 of the European Convention on Human Rights and Fundamental Freedoms, which recognises the right to life.[2]

47.   The protection afforded by the Charter in the field of health and safety at work actually extends beyond the workplace itself, contributing to the quality of the environment in general and therefore to the right to health enshrined in Article 11.[3]

48.   The Charter guarantees the right to health and safety at work by imposing the following obligations on the states:

–   "to issue safety and health regulations" (Article 3 para. 1) and "to provide for the enforcement of such regulations by measures of supervision" (Article 3 para. 2). Other provisions of the Charter supplement these measures; Article 2 para. 4, for example, provides for the adoption of specific measures (reduced working hours or additional paid holidays) where workers are engaged in dangerous or unhealthy occupations as prescribed (see Part III above). Articles 7 and 8 provide for the adoption and effective application of special measures to protect the health of children and women;

–   "to consult, as appropriate, employers' and workers' organisations on measures intended to improve industrial safety and health" (Article 3 para. 3). Article 3 paras. 1b and 1d of the Additional Protocol supplement this provision by requiring the Contract-

---

[1] Conclusions I, p. 22.

[2] General introduction to Conclusions XIV-2, p. 36.

[3] Conclusions V, p. xvii.

ing Parties to adopt measures enabling workers or their representatives to contribute to the protection of health and safety within the undertaking and to the supervision of the observance of regulations on these matters.

I.   Regulations on health and safety at work

49.   Article 3 para. 1 requires the Contracting Parties to issue safety and health regulations. The content and personal scope of these regulations must meet certain conditions in order to comply with the Charter.

A.   *Material content*

1.   *Health hazards covered*

a.   Reference to international technical standards

50.   The Charter does not specify which risks must be regulated under Article 3 para. 1. The Committee's supervision is indirect, through reference to international technical standards on occupational safety and health. It recently mentioned the existence of *"a very complete set of international technical reference standards which can be of use for defining and listing the main risks and occupations concerning which regulations should provide for protection and prevention measures in order to comply with Article 3 para. 1 of the Charter".*[1]

51.   The international reference standards concerned are all the ILO health and safety conventions and the numerous Community directives covering most aspects of the protection of the health and safety at work.[2]

52.   While the Committee's references to the numerous ILO conventions go back over a number of supervision cycles, its systematic reference to Community law is more recent (supervi-

---

[1] General introduction to Conclusions XIV-2, p. 37.

[2] A list of the relevant texts is given in Appendix VII.

sion cycle XIV-2). This has become necessary in the Committee's opinion because of the substantial development of Community law in recent years, ie since the Single European Act (1986) added Article 118A to the Treaty Establishing the European Community, concerning improvements to health and safety conditions in the working environment,[1] and the subsequent adoption in December 1989 of the Community Charter of the fundamental rights of workers.

b.   Risks concerned

53.   The Committee makes an overall assessment of the cover provided by the regulations. However, it requires that these include rules concerning "most risks". If the Committee finds that the measures in force fulfil this requirement it concludes that from this point of view the situation complies with Article 3 para. 1.[2] If it observes that no regulation has been issued concerning a specific risk, it does not necessarily conclude that the situation is at variance with the Charter but looks at the overall situation while inviting the Contracting Party concerned to remedy any shortcomings.

54.   Reflecting the traditional structure of domestic laws and regulations, the Committee's supervision is organised in the following manner:

55.   First of all, it ascertains whether a framework law lays down the *general obligations incumbent on employers and workers* in respect of occupational safety and health. Such laws now exist in all the Parties to the Charter which are members of the European Union or Parties to the Agreement on the European Economic Area, subsequent in certain cases to the incorporation into domestic law of Framework Directive 89/391/EC on the introduction of measures to encourage improvements in the safety and health of workers at work.

56.   The Committee then examines those regulations which lay down *specific obligations*. Aware of the particularly changing

---

[1] Now Article 137 of the revised treaty.

[2] The Committee made this type of assessment for many states during supervision cycle XIV-2.

nature of regulations in this field with the progress made in technology, ergonomics and medicine, the Committee has said that it *"will explain the new areas to which it will turn its attention each time it examines Article 3"*.[1]

57.   It is essential for conformity with Article 3 para. 1 that the regulations take these developments into account. The distinctive feature of the field of Article 3 has to do with the appearance of new risks, e.g from new chemical products which are coming into use in industry and agriculture and which can present dangers to workers' health and safety that may reveal themselves only at a later stage. The Committee therefore pays particular attention to whether or not the Contracting Parties show that the existing regulations are still adequate and, if appropriate, adapt them continuously to the changes brought about by technical developments.[2]

58.   At this stage,[3] apart from those hazards related to work organisation which are covered by other provisions of the Charter,[4] the Committee verifies in connection with Article 3 that regulations on the following risks exist:

i.   Establishment, alterations and upkeep of workplaces – Work equipment

  –   Workplaces and equipment, in particular machine protection, manual load handling, screen work

  –   Hygiene (commerce and offices)

  –   Maximum weight

---

[1] General introduction to Conclusions XIV-2, p. 37.

[2] Conclusions III, p. 17; addendum to Conclusions XI-2, Ireland, p. 14.

[3] Supervision cycle XIV-2, reference period 1992-96.

[4] Those concerning working hours, a weekly rest period, holidays with pay, etc, which come under Article 2, the purpose of which, like Article 3, is to protect the health and safety of workers. The Committee considers that verifying the impact of working hours and particularly changes in working hours (flexibility measures) on the health and safety of workers falls within the scope of Article 2 (see paragraphs 18 to 28 above). Under the revised Charter its supervision work in this respect will extend to the special measures to be taken in the event of night work (Article 2 para. 7).

- Air pollution, noise and vibration
- Personal protective equipment
- Safety and/or health signs at work.

ii. Hazardous agents and substances

- Chemical, physical and biological agents, particularly carcinogens, including: white lead (paints), benzene, asbestos, vinyl chloride monomer, metallic lead and its ionic compounds, ionising radiation;
- Control of major accident hazards involving dangerous substances

iii. Risks connected with certain sectors or activities

- Marking of weight on packages transported by vessels
- Protection of dockers against accidents
- Dock work
- Building safety provisions, temporary or mobile construction sites
- Mining, mineral extraction by drilling in open quarries and underground mines
- Ships and fishing vessels
- Prevention of major industrial accidents

The Committee also checks that risks in the farming and transport sectors are regulated.

iv. Risks connected with certain particularly vulnerable categories of workers

- Risks related to type of work and occupational status

59.   There have been substantial changes in the characteristics of the active population in recent years, and in particular an increase in the use of insecure types of employment (such as temporary and fixed-term employment). The Committee has observed that these workers are more exposed to a combination of health and safety

risks related both to the nature of the work they are asked to do (often in the building and industrial sectors) and to their status.[1]

60.   This explains why the Committee decided, in supervision cycle XIV-2, systematically to verify the regulations applicable to these categories of workers. It has already established that they should enjoy the same level of health protection at work as other workers in the same firm and that suitable rules must be laid down to take account of the specific nature of this type of employment relationship, for example by drawing up a list of occupations in which these workers may not be employed, or providing for them to receive special information, training and medical surveillance.[2]

–   Risks connected with the age and condition of health of workers

61.   In addition to the general provisions of Article 3 para. 1, two provisions of the Charter define specific measures to be taken to guarantee the right of children and young persons to protection (Article 7) and the right of employed women to protection, particularly pregnant women and nursing mothers (Article 8 para. 4). The Committee has decided to examine compliance with these specific health and safety provisions in the context of the articles concerned:[3]

---

[1] General introduction to Conclusions XIV-2, pp. 38 and 39. See in particular the situation in France: the Committee expressed concern at the high incidence of industrial accidents among temporary workers (Conclusions XIII-1, p. 86). It was subsequently able to examine the legislation applicable to the health and safety of these workers in detail, and found *"French regulations satisfactory in view of their adaptation to cater for the specific features of temporary or atypical employment. In various respects, they ensure better protection than is prescribed by European Community law"*. (Conclusions XIV-2, p. 288).

[2] The Committee has already detected shortcomings in the Irish and Spanish legislation (*ibid.*, pp. 390 and 675 respectively).

[3] General introduction to Conclusions XIV-2, p. 39. For example, having noted a gap in Swedish legislation on the protection of pregnant women or nursing mothers from exposure to white lead, the Committee decided that as far as the Charter was concerned this question was covered by Article 8 para. 4, which Sweden had not accepted, rather than by Article 3 para. 1 (Conclusions XIV-2, p. 704).

62. Article 7 of the Charter contains provisions for specific measures to be taken in relation to children and young persons: minimum age of admission to employment with the exception of certain prescribed light work, higher minimum age for certain dangerous and unhealthy occupations, limited working hours under 18 years of age, ban on night work under 18 years of age, special medical surveillance. The Committee's case law on this subject is presented in detail in the monograph on *Children and adolescents in the European Social Charter.*[1]

63. Article 8 para. 4 of the Charter requires the Contracting Parties to regulate the employment of women workers on night work in industrial employment (Article 8 para. 4a) and to prohibit the employment of women workers in underground mining and, as appropriate, in all other work which is unsuitable for them by reason of its dangerous, unhealthy or arduous nature (para. 4.b). The Committee has accepted for several supervision cycles that states confine this prohibitions to situations connected with maternity, ie. *"to protect motherhood, notably pregnancy, confinement and the post-natal period, as well as future children".*[2] The Committee's case law on this subject is presented in detail in the recent monograph on *Equality between women and men in the European Social Charter* (1998).[3]

2. Level of prevention and protection required

a. No major gaps

64. The Committee considers that the extent, technical nature and development of health and safety regulations prevent it from monitoring the situation in a detailed, thorough fashion. It therefore makes a global appraisal and has made it a principle that in order for regulations to meet the requirements of Article 3 para. 1 there must be no major gap in the prevention and protection provided against the risks listed above.[4]

---

[1] Social Charter monographs – No. 3.

[2] Conclusions X-2, pp. 97 and 98.

[3] Social Charter monographs – No. 2, new edition, pp. 51-59.

[4] Conclusions XIV-2, p. 40.

65.   As well as the information contained in the report, the Committee takes into consideration the observations of the ILO Committee of Experts on the Application of ILO Conventions and Recommendations in the field, as well as information about the incorporation of Community directives into the domestic law of Contracting Parties which are members of the European Union or Parties to the Agreement on the European Economic Area.

66.   The Committee attaches particular importance to the following:

  –   regulations which are sufficiently detailed:

67.   Legal provisions on occupational safety and health must be sufficiently detailed to be applied effectively and efficiently. For example, over the period from 1992 to 1996 the Committee noted a general policy on the part of the Norwegian authorities to abandon detailed legislation in favour of the general provisions of the Working Environment Act. It reminded the Government that the Charter requires Contracting Parties to have a sufficiently detailed legal and regulatory framework and said that it would monitor any changes in the next supervision cycle;[1]

  –   the importance of a particular activity in the country's economy and the number of workers engaged in that activity:

68.   The Committee expressed doubts about the level of safety regulations in the fishing industry in Portugal, for example, considering that "*in view of the fishing industry's importance in Portugal and the significant risks which the activity involves, any deficiency in the health and safety regulations can have serious consequences*". It therefore stressed that the following report should show that suitable, comprehensive and sufficiently stringent health and safety measures had been taken to protect fishing industry workers;[2]

  –   alignment of legislation with current knowledge as reflected in international reference standards:

---

[1] Conclusions XIV-2, Norway, p. 584. See also the situation in Austria, *ibid.*, p. 80, and Malta, Conclusions XIII-2, p. 249 and Conclusions XIV-2, p. 505.

[2] *Ibid.*, pp. 637 and 638.

69.   The Committee has emphasised, for example that it is important in terms of conformity with Article 3 para. 1 to set suitably low exposure limit values for benzene, in keeping with current standards as reflected in Community Directive 97/42, which, like ILO standards, recognises benzene as a carcinogenic agent present in a large number of work situations;[1]

–   trends in occupational accidents and diseases, which are examined in connection with Article 3 para. 2:

70.   This information gives the Committee a better picture of the situation in different countries and enables it to draw the attention of governments to those sectors or activities where high accident and disease rates may point to shortcomings in the legislation[2].

71.   When the Committee observes shortcomings in this respect, it suggests areas in which it considers improvements should be made and invites the government concerned to remedy the situation. The Committee has not yet found a situation to fail to comply with the Charter for this reason.

b.   Measures concerning exposure to asbestos and ionising radiation

72.   The Committee has been more specific in its definition of the type of prevention and protection required under Article 3 para. 1 in connection with certain specific risks, always with reference to international technical standards. Its appraisal of these particular risks plays a decisive role in its appreciation of the overall level of protection.

73.   Initially, the Committee decided to concentrate on protection against exposure to asbestos and ionising radiation. Accordingly, it asked a general question in Conclusions XIII-4 concerning the current situation of regulations in those Contracting Parties which

---

[1] *Ibid.*, Italy, p. 428, and Spain, p. 674.

[2] Conclusions XII-1, Denmark, p. 81; Conclusions, XIII-1, pp. 100 and 101, United Kingdom; Conclusions XIV-2, Belgium, p. 121, Germany, p. 300, Iceland, p. 367.

have accepted Article 3 para. 1[1] and examined the answers it received during supervision cycle XIV-2.

i.   Exposure to asbestos

74.   The international technical reference standards are ILO Convention No. 162 of 1986, on asbestos, and Community Directive 83/477, on the protection of workers from risks related to exposure to asbestos at work, as amended by Directive 91/382. The Committee also took note of the adoption by the Parliamentary Assembly of the Council of Europe of a recommendation on the dangers of asbestos for workers and the environment (Recommendation 1369 (1998)).

75.   In the light of the standards embodied in these documents the Committee considered that the Contracting Parties fully guaranteed the right of workers, under Article 3 of the Charter, to safe and healthy working conditions only if the following measures were adopted:[2]

---

[1] Conclusions XIII-4, p. 341: *"The Committee asked that all Contracting Parties having accepted Article 3 para. 1 submit information in their next reports on the measures taken to ensure effective protection of workers against ionising radiation, by reviewing maximum permissible doses of ionising radiation in the light of current knowledge as evidenced in particular by the recommendations, adopted in 1990 (Publication No. 60) on the basis of new physiological findings by the International Commission on Radiological Protection (ICRP).*

The Committee also drew the attention of the Contracting Parties having accepted Article 3 para. 1 to the question asked under Article 11 on protection against the risks connected with exposure to asbestos, which referred inter alia, to the protection of the health of workers against such risks".

The question under Article 11 (the right to protection of health) to which the Committee referred was worded as follows: *"the Committee asked that all Contracting Parties having accepted Article 11 submit information in their next reports on measures taken to ensure the effective protection of the health of their population against the risks connected with exposure to asbestos, either in their occupational activity or in the general environment in which they are living, in particular in their accommodation and in public buildings."* (Conclusions XIII-4, p. 116).

[2] General introduction to Conclusions XIV-2, pp. 41 and 42.

– asbestos exposure limit levels at least equal to or lower than the limits set in the Directive:

76. The Committee noted in this respect that the ILO Convention and the Directive provide for the prescription of limits to exposure, and that the Directive sets them at 0.6 fibres per cm^3 for chrysolite (ribbon fibres considered only slightly dangerous) and at 0.3 fibres per cm^3 for the other types of asbestos. It also noted that the ILO Convention requires limits to be revised and periodically updated in keeping with technological progress and developments in technical and scientific knowledge.

77. The Committee found in the course of supervision cycle XIV-2 that these requirements were met in all the member states of the European Union except Greece. It accordingly informed the Greek Government that, subject to whatever changes might occur in the meantime, it would bear this shortcoming in mind in its appraisal of conformity with Article 3 para. 1 during the next supervision cycle (XVI-2, reference period 1997-2000);[1]

– a ban on the use at workplaces of asbestos in one of its most harmful forms (crocidolite, straight blue fibres):

78. Although Article 3 para. 1 does not call for the total prohibition of asbestos, the Committee has held that this "is a measure which will ensure that the right provided under Article 3 para. 1 of the Charter is more effectively guaranteed".[2] The ILO Convention requires that when necessary and technically possible, legislation should provide for the replacement by other, less toxic materials or the partial prohibition of the use of asbestos, while the Parliamentary Assembly's recommendation states that asbestos must be eliminated where technical knowledge allows.

79. The Committee has therefore welcomed the steps taken by several Contracting Parties having accepted Article 3 para. 1 to prohibit the use of asbestos, while noting that the measures differ considerably in terms of the scope of the ban (use, handling, import, export, sale and/or manufacture), the exceptions allowed and the types of fibre which are prohibited.

---

[1] Conclusions XIV-2, Greece p. 334.

[2] General introduction to Conclusions XIV-2, p. 41.

- drawing up an inventory of all contaminated buildings and materials. This requirement shows the broader context of Article 3 para. 1, beyond the work place proper, namely the right of the whole population to a healthy environment. The Committee does not require the immediate treatment of all contaminated buildings. The Parties are free to decide what action to take and the Committee examines the results achieved.

ii.   Exposure to ionising radiation

80.   The Committee considers that in order to comply with Article 3 para. 1 the Contracting Parties must provide effective protection against the risks related to ionising radiation. The protective measures taken must be in keeping with current knowledge as reflected in the latest recommendations of the International Commission on Radiological Protection (ICRP publication No. 60, 1990).[1] *Inter alia* these recommendations set limit levels for occupational exposure and for occasional exposure of persons not working directly with radioactive substances.

81.   The ILO Committee of experts takes these recommendations into consideration in its appraisal of compliance with ILO Convention No. 115 on radiation protection. They are also reflected in the dose levels recommended in Directive 96/29/Euratom, establishing basic standards on health protection of individuals against the dangers of ionising radiation.

82.   Having noted during supervision cycle XIV-2 that numerous Contracting States had not yet aligned their legislation with the ICRP recommendation, the Committee urged them to do so before the end of the next reference period (1997-2000) and invited states which are members of the European Union or Parties to the Agreement on the European Economic Area to do so in the framework of the incorporation into domestic law of Directive 96/29/Euratom.

---

[1] *Ibid.*, p. 42.

B. Workers and sectors protected

83. All workers without exception, whatever their status and sector of activity, must be covered by regulations on health and safety at work. Article 33 of the Charter does not apply to Article 3.[1]

84. In the early supervision cycles the Committee made it quite clear that *"this article being designed to guarantee the right to safe and healthy working conditions not only for employed persons but also for the self-employed, ought to apply to all sectors of the economy if only on account of the technical advances and increasing mechanisation manifest in every branch of activity".*[2]

85. To simplify things, the Committee deals separately in its case law with the personal and material scope. These two aspects of Article 3 para. 1 are interrelated, however, and the same question can often be viewed from either angle. This applies, for example, to workers at risk (such as temporary workers) or occupied in high-risk fields of activity (such as the construction industry).

1. All economic sectors

86. All sectors of the economy must be covered by the regulations:[3] manufacturing industry, mining and quarrying, commerce and transport (including shipping) and agriculture, as well as the

---

[1] Article 33 stipulates that the commitments taken on by Contracting Parties in respect of certain provisions of the Charter shall be regarded as effectively fulfilled if the provisions are applied "to the great majority of the workers concerned".

[2] Conclusions II, p. 12.

[3] Conclusions I, pp. 22 and 173. On p. 22 the Committee considered *"that a country which has accepted this Article can only be regarded as fulfilling the undertaking deriving from it if it can prove that safety and health regulations have been issued for all economic sectors"*.

public sector.[1] Consequently, when health and safety regulations do not apply to a particular sector the Committee concludes that the situation is not in conformity with Article 3 para. 1.[2]

87.   In order to ensure that all sectors are indeed covered, the Committee expects the texts to be sufficiently specific and clearly state which sectors are covered.[3] This does not mean that specific legislation must be passed for each activity or sector, but the wording of the texts must be sufficiently specific to permit their effective application in all sectors, bearing in mind the degree of risk in different sectors.[4]

88.   The Committee also checks that sectors are fully covered[5] and that all firms are covered, regardless of how many people they employ.[6]

89.   As was explained earlier with regard to the conditions relating to the material content of the regulations (see paragraph 58 sub-paragraph *iii* above), the Committee attaches particular impor-

---

[1] The Charter applies to both the public and the private sectors. Since Governments often forget to state whether health and safety regulations also apply to the public sector or whether special regulations exist, the Committee always asks the question. For recent examples, see Conclusions XIII-3, Portugal, p. 255, Conclusions XIV-2, Malta p. 506.

[2] For example, the Committee concluded that the situation in Ireland was not in conformity with the Charter as there were no full and systematic regulations governing health and safety in agriculture (see Conclusions II, p. 12 to Conclusions VI, p. 15; this particular shortcoming was subsequently remedied but the conclusion remained negative for other reasons); the same applied in Cyprus, where there were no safety regulations in the agricultural sector (see Conclusions III, p. 19; the situation has since been remedied).

[3] See, for example, addendum to Conclusions XIII-3, Luxembourg, p. 26.

[4] Conclusions, XIV-2, Portugal, p. 637.

[5] See, for example, in the public sector: Conclusions XIII-1, Spain, p. 90 (health and safety measures in the police); Conclusions XIII-3, Portugal, p. 255 (measures in public security and emergency services such as the armed forces and that police and other civil protection services).

[6] See, for example, Conclusions XIII-1, Greece, pp. 86 and 87: noting that minimum staff levels were still required for the application of occupational health and safety measures, the Committee renewed its negative conclusion. Since supervision cycle XIII-3 the situation has been remedied.

tance to the prevention and protection measures taken against the risks inherent in certain activities, such as construction, fishing and transport. Conversely it has accepted derogations in respect of certain categories of workers for practical reasons, such as the low risk in certain economic sectors. It did point out, however, that this did not apply to agriculture.[1]

2. All workers

90. Occupational health and safety regulations must protect all workers, whatever their legal status.

a. Employees and self-employed workers

91. Unlike other provisions of the Charter, such as Article 2, which concerns only those workers with an employment contract, the Committee decided from the outset that, because of its context, the term "workers" as used in Article 3 did not cover employees only.[2] This provision of the Charter therefore requires regulations to be set in place both for employees and for the self-employed.

92. In the early supervision cycles, the Committee noted that the main shortcomings in terms of the personal scope of national regulations concerned the lack of proper protection for self-employed people, a situation it invariably found to be in breach of the Charter.[3] The Committee has acknowledged that the incorporation into domestic law of Community directives in matters

---

[1] Conclusions IV, p. 22.

[2] Conclusions I, p. 8; Conclusions II, p. 182.

[3] In more recent supervision cycles the Committee reached negative conclusions for this reason in respect of Belgium (Conclusions XIII-4, p. 342; it subsequently revised its judgment in the light of information supplied in supervision cycle XIV-2, Conclusions XIV-2, pp. 122 to 124); Italy (the situation has been negative for this reason since Conclusions II; the Committee of Ministers sent a recommendation – No. R ChS (95) 8 – to the Italian Government during supervision cycle XIII-1; see, most recently, Conclusions XIV-2, pp. 429 and 430); Greece (Conclusions XIII-3, p. 205; the Committee subsequently found that the situation had improved and deferred its assessment in Conclusions XIV-2, pp. 335 and 336); the Netherlands (the conclusion has been negative for this reason since Conclusions IX-1, see most recently Conclusions XIV-2, pp. 542 and 543).

ration into domestic law of Community directives in matters of health and safety at work has led several Contracting Parties to extend the personal scope of their regulations.[1] Unlike the Charter, however, Community law does not apply to self-employed workers as such.[2] So in this respect the Charter goes further than Community law.

93.   Several reasons prompted the Committee to maintain this interpretation:

–   discrimination between employed and self-employed workers as regards safety and health at work would hardly be compatible with the concern to ensure a satisfactory working environment for all workers, especially where employed and self-employed workers are employed on the same work, which they frequently are on hazardous work sites such as building sites;[3]

–   the activities of the self-employed can also affect the health and safety of others, for example when they use the same workplace as other workers (who are not employees of the self-employed persons concerned) – family members, unpaid helpers, employees of contractors, maintenance staff, etc.[4]

94.   These are decisive factors in the Committee's assessment of the situation of self-employed workers: the Charter requires the working environment to be danger-free and healthy in order to protect the health and safety of all workers. This is the yardstick by which it measures the degree of protection enjoyed by self-employed workers.[5] The Committee has nevertheless pointed out

---

[1] General introduction to Conclusions XIV-2, p. 43.

[2] Directive 89/391 covers workers in the sense of any person employed by an employer, including trainees and apprentices, but excluding "domestic servants" and employers in the sense of "any natural or legal person who has an employment relationship with the worker and has responsibility for the undertaking and/or establishment" (Article 3a and b).

[3] Conclusions III, p. 17.

[4] Conclusions IV, p. 21.

[5] The Committee has acknowledged that *"given the difference in the conditions in which an employee and a self-employed worker carry out their activities, there may, to a certain extent, have to be different rules for applying safety and health requirements. However, the objective of providing a safe*

that the obligation incumbent on self-employed workers in certain countries to join a special insurance scheme against occupational accidents is not a sufficient measure for conformity with Article 3 para. 1.[1]

95.   The Committee took these considerations into account when examining the new Belgian legislation (Act of 4 August 1996 on the welfare of workers at work). It noted that although the category of the self-employed was still not fully protected, the rules on prevention and safety provided for in the 1996 Act had to be respected in the majority of situations in which the health and safety of such workers might be jeopardised. The only self-employed workers to whom the law did not apply at all were those who worked for themselves, at home, without anyone under their authority, so the Committee was able to conclude that Belgium guaranteed self-employed workers the protection required under Article 3 para. 1.[2]

96.   Finally, the legal distinction between "employed" workers and "self-employed" workers can sometimes be rather vague, when the latter category are in fact "false self-employed workers" working under the authority of somebody else even if there is no employment contract. This explains why the Committee is attentive to the definition of the persons covered and makes sure that all persons working under the authority of another person are protected, regardless of whether they are bound by an employment contract.[3] In particular the Committee verifies the situation of workers employed in family concerns without being paid wages, and that of self-employed sub-contractors.[4]

---

and healthy working environment must be the same for employed and self-employed workers and the regulations and their enforcement must be adequate and suitable in view of the work being done" (Conclusions XIII-1, Netherlands, p. 89: Conclusions XIII-4, Belgium, p. 342).

[1] Conclusions XIV-2, Luxembourg, pp. 470 and 471, and Spain, pp. 675 and 676.

[2] *Ibid.*, Belgium, p. 123. The Committee used the same reasoning in the case of Austria, in Conclusions V, p. 19. See also the situations in Greece and the Netherlands in Conclusions XIV-2, pp. 335 and 336, and pp. 542 and 543.

[3] For example: Conclusions XIV-2, Belgium, pp. 122 and 123.

[4] For example, *ibid.*, France, p. 263.

b. Domestic employees and home workers

97. No workplace, even the home, must be "exempt" from the safety and health regulations provided for in Article 3 of the Charter. It has often come to the Committee's notice, however, that workers employed in the home – domestic employees and people working at home – enjoy little protection if any. It therefore makes a point of verifying the regulations applied to these workers.[1]

98. The Committee does not object to the regulations being adapted to the type of activity and the relative safety of this type of work or to them being worded in fairly general terms.[2]

II. Effective enforcement of safety and health regulations

99. Under paragraph 2 of Article 3 states are required to provide for the enforcement of safety and health regulations through measures of supervision. The purpose of this provision is to guarantee effective enjoyment of the right to safe and healthy working conditions.

100. The Committee has given a broad scope to this provision: in appraising compliance it takes into account not only the existence of a system of inspection and sanctions but also trends in occupational accidents and diseases. In the case law these factors are key signs of effective application of safety and health regulations.

101. As its wording suggests, paragraph 2 supplements the obligation embodied in paragraph 1. As the two paragraphs go together, the obligation laid down in paragraph 2 covers the same workers and the same sectors of activity as paragraph 1: measures to supervise the enforcement of safety and health regulations

---

[1] In Conclusions XIII-1 (p. 85) the Committee asked all States bound by paragraph 1 and/or 2 of Article 3 *"to indicate, in their next report, the extent to which home workers are covered by the regulations governing health and safety at work and the measures which exist for the supervision of the enforcement of such regulations"*.

[2] See, for example, the situation of domestic employees in Belgium, which the Committee found to be in conformity with Article 3 para. 1 (Conclusions XIV-2, p. 123).

must exist for all workers and all sectors of activity.[1] Initially, the Committee considered that these two provisions were so closely related that its conclusions in respect of each of them should be the same. Thus, when a situation was at variance with paragraph 1 because self-employed workers did not enjoy proper protection, it invariably concluded that the situation in respect of paragraph 2 was not in conformity with the Charter.[2] Recently, however, focusing more on the content of the obligations, the Committee has revised its position and has considered, since supervision cycle XIV-2, that "*each of these provisions contains its own requirements which may be the subject of an independent assessment*".[3]

A.   Trends in occupational accident and disease rates

102.   In order to assess overall trends, the Committee takes into account the number of injuries in absolute terms and the change in the number of workers over the same period,[4] which enables it to calculate the injury rate (number of injuries per hundred workers). Since supervision cycle XIV-2, the Committee has adopted a "comparative" approach. To do so, in addition to the information contained in the reports, it uses Eurostat statistics on accidents in the European Union and the *Yearbook of Labour Statistics* produced by the ILO.

103.   The number and progression of fatal accidents in relation to total accidents is an essential factor of compliance with this provision of the Charter.[5]

---

[1] The general observations made by the Committee in Conclusions II, p. 12, III, p. 17 and IV, p. 21 concern Article 3 as a whole (see paragraphs 57, 84 and 93 above).

[2] Conclusions I, p. 23. See, most recently: Conclusions XIII-3, Greece, p. 209, Italy, p. 211, Netherlands, p. 212, and Conclusions XIII-4, Belgium, p. 344.

[3] General introduction to Conclusions XIV-2, p. 43.

[4] If there is no mention in the report of the number of workers taken into consideration for statistical purposes, the Committee refers to total employment as defined and reported in the *ILO Yearbook of Labour Statistics*.

[5] In the case of Belgium, for example, the Committee expressed concern that the frequency of fatal accidents has remained stable since the beginning of

104.   The Committee is aware of the problems linked to the reliability of statistics in general and to statistical comparisons in particular. It has observed substantial divergences in several states between the number of accidents declared and the number that actually occurred, seriously impairing the use of statistics as a tool.[1] For this reason, it has only found breaches of the Charter where situations present obvious problems.

105.   The Committee found, for example, that the number of industrial accidents and fatalities recorded in Portugal was far higher than average in the European Union, and that the situation had not improved during the reference period. It considered that the frequency of industrial accidents and fatalities was clearly too high in Portugal for it to conclude that effective exercise of the right to health and safety at work was ensured.[2] So far this is the only case of non-conformity with Article 3 para. 2 on these grounds.

106.   The Committee examines the trend in every sector of the economy and closely examines those sectors with high accident rates. It has noted in this respect that in the great majority of Contracting Parties, the construction sector of activity remains the most dangerous: the average rate of accidents and fatal accidents is twice as high there as in other branches. The Committee is aware that temporary workers and sub-contractors are often present in this sector, where the labour turnover is rapid.[3] It feels that these factors in part explain the high number of accidents and

---

the 1980s while the quality and quantity of protective and preventive measures have steadily increased (Conclusions XIV-2, p. 125).

[1] See also the questions put to the Netherlands in Conclusions XIV-2, p. 544.

[2] Conclusions XIV-2, Portugal, p. 640.

[3] General introduction to Conclusions XIV-2, p. 45. See, in particular, the situation in Spain (*ibid.*, p. 677): the Committee drew the government's attention to the fact that the construction industry was the worst-hit sector in terms of industrial accidents during the reference period 1992-1996, and that one reason could be the very high proportion of temporary workers in the sector (47% of all construction workers) and the very frequent use of sub-contractors. The Committee informed the government that the adoption of measures to improve the situation would be a key criterion in its assessment of conformity with Article 3 para. 2 in the next supervision cycle (cycle XVI-2, reference period 1997-2000).

confirm the importance of information and training for all workers in general and, above all, the necessity of devising appropriate information and training methods for workers in insecure employment (see paragraphs 59 and 60 above).

107.   The Committee also examines the distribution of industrial accidents according to size of firm and has noted on several occasions that the number of accidents in small firms is proportionally higher than in large firms. Where this is the case, it endeavours to establish why and recommends that steps be taken to curb this trend. It observed this phenomenon in France, in firms employing fewer than fifty people, and related it to the fact that health, safety and working conditions committees were compulsory in France only in firms with more than fifty employees.[1]

108.   The Committee has not yet established criteria for assessing occupational disease trends. The main problem is the lapse of time that can pass between the appearance of the risk, its identification and the declaration of the illness, or even its recognition. The Committee recently observed an increase in deaths in France subsequent to complaints caused by asbestos dust. It acknowledged that while France had delayed in taking adequate measures, current regulations included the main elements of protection and prevention in relation to asbestos. It had no alternative but to hope that the effects of these measures on the incidence of asbestos-related complaints would become apparent during future supervision cycles.[2]

---

[1] Conclusions XIII-1, France, p. 95, and Conclusions XIV-2, p. 266. See also: *ibid.*, Belgium, pp. 125 and 126.

[2] *Ibid.*, France, pp. 261 (Article 3 para. 1) and 265 (Article 3 para. 2).

B.   Supervision of the enforcement of regulations[1]

1.   Labour inspection system

109.   All Contracting Parties to the Charter are bound, under Article 20 para. 5, to maintain a system of labour inspection "appropriate to national conditions". The Charter thus imposes no particular model for the inspection system, so the systems may differ considerably from one country to another.

110.   The Committee takes into account the following factors when assessing the efficacy of the inspection system.

a.   Power of the labour inspectors

111.   The Committee asks each Contracting Party to describe the administrative organisation of the inspection service, the fields of activity covered and the establishments subject to inspection. The Committee makes sure, in keeping with the scope of Article 3 para. 2, that the inspectors are empowered to inspect all work places in all sectors of activity.

112.   The work places concerned include the home, in order to guarantee the effective enjoyment of safe and healthy working conditions to domestic employees and home workers and also to self-employed people working from home.

b.   Activities of the inspection services

113.   This is the most useful piece of information for the Committee in making its assessment. It takes into the account the number of inspections made and the percentage of workers covered by the

---

[1] The Committee regularly invites those states which are parties to ILO Convention No. 81 concerning Labour Inspection in Industry and Commerce and/or Convention No. 129 on Labour Inspection to send it copies of the reports they periodically submit to the ILO on the application of these conventions (see, for example, the general question asked in Conclusions XIII-1, p. 93). The information contained in these reports is generally sufficient for the Committee to assess the situation in respect of labour inspection and sanctions.

visits. Without this information, the Committee is unable to adopt a conclusion.[1]

114. Compliance with Article 3 para. 2 requires the Contracting Parties to show that *"a minimum number of inspections are performed on a regular basis, the aim being to ensure that the right enshrined in Article 3 is effectively enjoyed by the largest possible number of workers".*[2] In the case of Portugal the Committee found that the inspection rate, taken as the ratio of workers inspected to total employment, was so low that this objective could not be considered to be achieved. It therefore concluded that the situation did not comply with the requirements of Article 3 para. 2.[3]

115. It is important from the standpoint of Article 3 para. 2 that work-site inspections should serve to *monitor* the application of occupational safety and health regulations. Having observed a declining trend in inspections over the recent supervision cycles, sometimes offset by an increase in inspectors' prevention activities, the Committee stressed that, although necessary, prevention activities should not be developed to the detriment of work-site inspections.[4]

---

[1] Over several supervision cycles the Committee concluded that Italy was not in conformity with this provision for lack of statistical information on the inspection activities of the Local Health Centres. The Committee also issued several recommendations to Italy on this subject (Recommendations Nos. R ChS (94) 4, supervision cycle XII-2, and R ChS (95) 7, supervision cycle XIII-1, reiterated in Resolution ChS (97) 1, supervision cycle XIII-3). In Conclusions XIV-2 the committee noted with satisfaction that the situation was changing.

[2] General introduction to Conclusions XIV-2, p. 46.

[3] *Ibid.*, Portugal, p. 642.

[4] General introduction to Conclusions XIV-2, p. 45. This was brought to the attention of the Austrian Government, for example, whose reports revealed a 50% decrease in the number of inspection visits in the space of ten years, and a simultaneous increase in the advisory activities of the inspectors (Conclusions XI-2, pp. 61 and 62, Conclusions XII-2, p. 72 and Conclusions XIV-2, p. 84).

c.   Labour Inspectorate staff and means

116.   In order for the inspection system to be effective, inspection authorities must have the necessary means to conduct their activities. The Committee therefore monitors inspection staff figures to ensure that there are enough inspectors to carry out regular visits in sufficient numbers, with enough time spent on each visit to make a thorough inspection.

117.   According to the statistics on the work of the Medical Inspectorate in Belgium, for example, the Committee noted that each inspector visits an average of 250 undertakings per year, and that it would therefore take 15 years on average for all undertakings to be inspected at least once. It doubted, under these circumstances, that the largest possible number of workers effectively benefited from the right enshrined in Article 3.[1]

118.   The Committee also takes an interest in the means of investigation open to inspectors and the action they can take, particularly when they consider that there is an imminent threat to workers' health or safety. It considers that the stoppage of activities, the placing of seals, etc., are appropriate means of action.[2]

119.   Another factor that influences the Committee's appraisal is the measures taken with a view to maintaining the competence of inspectors, taking account of technological and legal developments.[3] On the strength of the information supplied in supervision cycle XIV-2, the Committee found that most of the Contracting Parties complied with the requirements of Article 3 para. 2 in this respect.

---

[1] Conclusions XIV-2, Belgium, p. 128. The Committee nevertheless deferred its assessment on this point pending further information on the activities of another inspection authority.

[2] General introduction to Conclusions XIV-2, p. 46. See also Austria and Belgium, *ibid.*, pp. 84 and 128 respectively.

[3] General question asked in Conclusions XIII-1, p. 93.

2.   Sanctions

120.   The effectiveness of the enforcement of Article 3 para. 2 is also measured in terms of the deterrent effect on employers of the sanctions applicable in the event of failure to apply health and safety regulations. To establish this the Committee needs the following information:

–   the offences detected by the inspection authorities, the fields of activity concerned and what action was taken, including judicial proceedings;

–   the scale of penalties applied, broken down where applicable into administrative and criminal sanctions.

The Committee takes various criteria into account when assessing compliance from this angle:

–   the proportion of offences identified that give rise to sanctions;[1]

–   the connection between the frequency of infringements of the regulations and the severity of the penalties imposed;[2]

–   the overall level of sanctions[3] and how they are determined, for example whether they are proportional to the number of workers affected.[4]

III.   Consultation of and participation by workers and/or their representatives in occupational safety and health issues

121.   Under Article 3 para. 3 the Contracting Parties are required, as appropriate, to consult employers' and workers' organisations

---

[1] For example: Conclusions XIII-3, Greece, p. 209; Conclusions XIV-2, Belgium, p. 128.

[2] For example: Conclusions XII-1, Denmark and Sweden, pp. 82 and 86 respectively.

[3] For example: Cyprus, Conclusions XI-2, p. 63, and Conclusions XIV-2, p. 167; *ibid.*, Ireland, pp. 392 and 393.

[4] For example: *ibid.*, Denmark, p. 189.

on measures intended to improve industrial safety and health. Article 3 of the 1988 Additional Protocol to the Charter further provides for workers or their representatives to contribute to the determination and the improvement of working conditions and the working environment and, in particular, to the protection of health and safety (para. 1*b*) and the supervision of the observance of regulations on these measures (para. 1*d*).

A.   At national and regional level

1.   Consultation machinery and procedures

122.   The Contracting Parties must ensure that machinery and procedures exist for the public authorities to consult professional organisations, ie. trade unions and employers' organisations. Like the other paragraphs of Article 3, this obligation applies to all sectors of the economy, including the public sector.[1]

123.   The Committee considers that Contracting Parties meet this requirement where there are one or more bodies made up of representatives of government, employers' organisations[2] and workers' organisations which are consulted by the public authorities.[3] These bodies may be permanent or *ad hoc* bodies.

124.   Consultation must take place not only at the national level but also at regional level. Initially the Committee considered this as

---

[1] The more important the branch of activity, the more attention the Committee pays to it (eg the agricultural sector in France, Conclusions V, p. 23, and maritime activities in Norway, Conclusions XIV-2, p. 589).

[2] Having learned that the Danish Confederation of Employers had decided to withdraw from the Working Environment Council, the committee drew the Danish Government's attention to the fact that this situation would endanger the consultation required by Article 3 para. 3 (Conclusions XIV-2, p. 190).

[3] Such organisations exist in a large majority of the Contracting Parties which have accepted Article 3 para. 3, whatever their legal tradition, such as the Higher Council for the Prevention of Occupational Hazards set up in France in 1978, the National Council for Health and Safety at Work set up in Portugal by Legislative Decree No. 441/91, or the National Board of Occupational Safety and Health set up in Sweden under the provisions of Work Environment Act No. 1160 of 1977.

an essential condition of conformity with Article 3 para. 3.[1] It subsequently tempered its position. Having considered, in respect of Article 6 para. 1 of the Charter,[2] that special features of certain countries rendered regional tripartite organisations unnecessary,[3] its position on consultation with employers' and workers' organisations on measures to improve occupational health and safety is, *a fortiori*, the same.[4]

2. Content and frequency of consultation

125. Under the terms of the Charter, the obligation to consult management and labour is limited to "measures intended to improve industrial safety and health". It is clear from the case law that the Committee considers that the Contracting Parties fulfil their obligations in this respect if management and labour are consulted when occupational safety and health regulations are being prepared or revised. The public authorities may consult the social partners before or after preparing the draft texts.

126. The authorities must provide for consultation "as appropriate", i.e. *"whenever the need arises"*.[5] The frequency of consultations is therefore not left entirely to the discretion of the governments, but must follow changes in the regulations. The Committee has underlined that *"the rapid development of techniques and its consequences on security require a constant updating of health and safety regulations, which cannot be achieved without regular consultations with employers' and workers' organisations"*.[6] The Committee recently highlighted this requirement in the light of the particularly rapid development of health and safety regulations in the Contracting Parties members of the European

---

[1] Conclusions I, p. 23.

[2] Article 6 guarantees the right to bargain collectively, and paragraph 1 requires the Contracting Parities "to promote joint consultation between workers and employers".

[3] Conclusions XIII-2, Malta, p. 274.

[4] General introduction to Conclusions XIV-2, p. 48.

[5] Conclusions I, p. 24 and p. 174.

[6] See, for example: Conclusions V, p. 23, and Conclusions VII, p. xvii.

Union or Parties to the agreement on the European Economic Area, as a result of the incorporation of Community directives.[1]

127.   In order to verify that labour and management organisations are regularly consulted on changes to the regulations, the Committee requests information on the activities of the bodies responsible.[2]

B.   At enterprise level

1.   Consultation on occupational safety and health

128.   Under Article 3 para. 3 labour and management organisations must be consulted at enterprise level on any measures taken to improve health and safety, such as planning and introduction of new technologies.[3] This consultation must take place whenever the need arises (see paragraph 123 above).

129.   Without underestimating the importance of management and labour organisations within the enterprise, particularly in the field of health and safety, the Committee recently changed its approach concerning the consultation bodies. The change reflects a trend in the firm itself towards increased participation by workers or their representatives in the improvement of their working environment through specialised health and safety units (health and safety committees). The Committee considers that *"in setting up a specialist body representing workers' interests, which employers could consult in respect of health and safety measures, the right provided under Article 3 para. 3 of the Charter is more effectively guaranteed".*[4]

130.   Although governed by its own criteria, the right to consultation guaranteed under Article 3 para. 3 of the Charter is thus closely related to the right of workers, guaranteed by Article 3 of the Additional Protocol (see paragraphs 133 to 135 below), to take

---

[1] General introduction to Conclusions XIV-2, p. 47.

[2] The Contracting Parties are always asked what consultations have taken place and what subjects were covered.

[3] Addendum to Conclusion XIII-3, Luxembourg, p. 28.

[4] General introduction to Conclusions XIV-2, p. 48.

part in the determination and improvement of working conditions and the working environment.[1]

131.   It should be remembered that Article 33 of the Charter does not apply to Article 3 (see paragraph 83 above). Consequently, procedures for consulting workers or their representatives must exist in all enterprises within the scope of paragraph 3, and the Committee makes a point of ensuring that the number of employees firms must have in some states before they are obliged to set up health and safety committees does not deprive this provision of its substance.[2]

132.   Community Directive 89/391 on the introduction of measures to encourage improvements in the safety and health of workers at work introduced obligations on employers concerning the participation and consultation of workers (Article 11). The Committee expects the result to be an improvement in the situation in countries where there are customarily no instances for the consultation of workers' representatives in firms. Accordingly, it has asked the Contracting Parties what changes have been brought about by the incorporation of this text into domestic law.[3]

2.   *Participation in the determination and improvement of the work environment*

a.   Content of participation

133.   Article 3 para. 1 of the additional Protocol[4] requires the Parties to adopt or encourage measures enabling workers or their

---

[1] The Committee has generally considered that the information on the strength of which it assessed the conformity of the Parties to the Protocol was also sufficient for it to assess the situation of these countries with regard to Article 3 para. 3, which has a narrower scope (Conclusions XIV-2, Netherlands, Norway and Sweden, pp. 546, 589 and 711 respectively).

[2] The Committee noted, for example, that in Greece only those firms with 150 employees or more (ie a minority of firms) were obliged to set up occupational health and safety committees (EYAE), and asked how compliance with this provision was guaranteed in firms with fewer employees (Conclusions XIV-2, p. 340).

[3] General introduction to Conclusions XIV-2, p. 48.

[4] This has become Article 22 of the revised Charter.

representatives to contribute to the protection of health and safety within the undertaking (para. 1*b*) and to the supervision of the observance of regulations on these matters (para. 1*d*).

134.   Arrangements for such participation are made "in accordance with national legislation and practice". According to the appendix to the Protocol[1], this means that states may pass laws or issue regulations, or leave the matter to collective agreements, other agreements between employers and workers' representatives[2] or any other form of voluntary negotiation.

135.   The Protocol thus imposes no particular model of participation, which must simply be adequate and effective. In all the Contracting Parties whose cases the Committee has examined to date,[3] participation in the protection of health and safety at work subjects employers, at the very least, to the obligation to inform and consult workers or their representatives. In Sweden the participation procedure is more extensive, with an obligation on employers to conduct negotiations prior to making any decisions, and safety delegates or health and safety committees playing an important part in the decision-making process.[4]

136.   The role of workers or their representatives in participating in the "supervision of the observance" of health and safety regulations is not to replace the official supervisory bodies, but to ensure that their supervision is effective. According to the appendix to Article 3 of the Protocol, their contribution does not affect the powers and responsibilities of the bodies and authorities responsible for monitoring the application of the regulations.

---

[1] References to the provisions of the "appendix to the Protocol" concern Articles 2 and 3 of the Protocol.

[2] In Finland, for example, the subject matter of Article 3 is covered by collective agreements or other agreements concluded between employers and workers' representatives (Conclusions XIII-5, pp. 291 and 292).

[3] ie. Finland, Italy, the Netherlands, Norway and Sweden. Denmark should be submitting a report in June 1999 or March 2000 for supervision cycle XV-2. Greece and Slovakia are due to submit their reports in June 2001 or March 2002 for supervision cycle XVI-2.

[4] See the Conclusions adopted in respect of Articles 2 and 3 of the Protocol in Conclusions XIII-3, (pp. 445-448 and pp. 453 and 454), and XIII-5 (pp. 285-289 and pp. 299-302).

b. Participation structures

137. The right to participation may be exercised by workers and/or their representatives.

138. Like Article 3 of ILO Convention No. 135 concerning Protection and Facilities to be Afforded to Workers' Representatives in the Undertaking, the appendix to the Protocol stipulates that the term "workers' representatives" means persons who are recognised as such under national legislation or practice. They may therefore be union representatives or representatives freely elected by the workers in the firm.

139. In most cases the right guaranteed by this provision is exercised, depending on the size and/or activities of the undertaking, by one or more safety delegates elected by the workers, either directly or from union delegations, or by a health and safety committee on which management and labour are represented in equal numbers.

c. Effective participation

140. The right to participation must be accompanied by guarantees ensuring its effective exercise.[1] The Committee makes a point of asking the Contracting Parties what possibilities exist for workers or their representatives to lodge a complaint where their rights have been infringed.

d. Undertakings concerned

141. According to the appendix to the Protocol, the term "undertaking" is understood as "referring to a set of tangible and intangible components, with or without legal personality, formed to produce or provide services for financial gain and with power to determine its own market policy". Where applicable, ie. when an undertaking comprises various production units linked to a decision-making centre, the right to participation must exist in all the undertaking's establishments.

---

[1] General observation in Conclusions XIII-3, p. 440.

142.   The Committee has explained that it follows from the text that, in the public sector, only state-owned companies, or some of those companies, are concerned.[1] The public services proper fall outside the scope of Article 3.

143.   Also excluded, under the terms of the appendix to the Protocol, are religious communities and their institutions and, to such an extent as is necessary to protect the orientation of the undertaking, establishments pursuing activities which are inspired by certain ideals or guided by certain moral concepts, ideals and concepts which are protected by national legislation.[2]

144.   Under paragraph 2 of Article 3 the Parties may decide to limit the application of the right to participation to those undertakings which employ more than a certain number of workers. This makes it possible to allow for the different needs of firms according to their size, for example, by dispensing small firms from the need to make special arrangements to guarantee participation. The Committee therefore makes a point of asking the Contracting Parties where they draw the line.

145.   Finally, under the terms of Article 7 para. 2 of the Protocol the commitments deriving from Article 3 are regarded as effective if the provisions are applied "to the great majority of the workers concerned". Workers employed in undertakings which fall outside the scope of Article 3 because they have less than a certain number of employees are not taken into account in establishing the number of workers concerned (Appendix to Article 7). By analogy with its case law on Article 33 of the Charter,[3] the Committee considers that compliance with Article 3 of the Protocol exists where the proportion of workers who do not enjoy the right to participation is *"less than 20 % of the active population"*. "The great

---

[1] Conclusions XIII-3, Finland, p. 441, and Conclusions XIII-5, Norway, p. 284.

[2] According to the explanatory report (para. 68), this paragraph was inserted, *inter alia*, to meet the situation in the Federal Republic of Germany, where certain categories of undertakings with an "orientation" *(Tendenzbetriebe*, pursuing political, religious or educational aims) are excluded from the scope of the 1972 Act on the Organisation of Undertakings or from certain of its provisions. This exemption also applies to Sweden in respect of Article 2 (Conclusions XIII-5, p. 286).

[3] The wording of which is similar to that of Article 7 of the Protocol.

majority of the workers concerned" therefore means 80 %. In order to establish whether this is the case, the Committee needs to know the proportion of workers employed in private and public undertakings falling within the scope of Article 3 who enjoy the right to participation in the area covered by this provision.

C. Prospects

146. In view of its recent entry into force (1992), it is too early to take stock of the impact of the Protocol on the consultation and participation of workers and/or their representatives in the field of occupational safety and health. What can be said is that the entry into force of the revised Social Charter will enable the Committee to give more substance to the obligation of consultation embodied in Article 3 para. 3 of the Charter. The revised Charter effectively extends the obligation to consult employers' and workers' organisations to all those matters covered by Article 3 as amended: the formulation, implementation and periodical review of a "coherent national policy on occupational safety, occupational health and the working environment", the adoption and supervision of the enforcement of regulations in that field and promotion of the development of occupational health services.

Part three – Fair remuneration

147.   Article 4 of the Charter concerns the right to fair remuneration, an essential aspect of working life and one which the European Committee of Social Rights has applied with particular vigilance since the beginning. In addition to the right to a decent wage, laid down in the first paragraph, this Article also addresses the following fundamental aspects of wage protection: increased pay for overtime working, equal pay for work of equal value, reasonable periods of notice of termination of employment and the regulation of wage deductions.

148.   Since the rules and practices which apply to wage determination and protection may vary greatly from state to state, the text of Article 4 itself includes a final unnumbered paragraph permitting the rights involved to be implemented through collective agreements, statutory wage-fixing machinery or by other means appropriate to national conditions. This margin of discretion as to implementation means, for example, that states are not required to adopt a statutory minimum wage in order to comply with the first paragraph. However, the means adopted must be adequate and ensure full application of these provisions of the Charter. This may ultimately require the adoption of legislative rules, since reliance on collective agreements or custom must be sustained by a very exacting standard of proof.

I.   The right to a decent wage

149.   Under Article 4 para. 1, states undertake "to recognise the right of workers to a remuneration such as will give them and their families a decent standard of living".

150.   The importance of this guarantee is manifest. The Charter protects the essential rights interests of workers, ensuring that the conditions in which they work are reasonable and safe, and requiring a fair reward for their labour. Inadequate pay creates poverty traps, which may ensnare not just individuals and their families, but whole communities. Where unemployed persons have little or no

financial incentive to work, the very spirit of the Charter is contravened. Salaries which lag far behind average earnings are incompatible with social justice.

151. As stated above, this provision of the Charter does not imply the introduction of statutory minimum wages in all Contracting States. It nevertheless lays down a standard in the field of wage determination which governments are bound to respect. Since the first supervision cycle, the Committee has sought to investigate the reality of low pay with a view to determining whether the state obligation under Article 4 para. 1 was being met. This assessment has always been problematic due to, *inter alia*, differing socio-economic contexts across the countries concerned and the difficulty in obtaining adequate data on incomes and the cost of living. In response to these difficulties, the Committee's assessment method has evolved considerably over the years.

152. The text of the provision itself refers to remuneration "such as will give [workers] and their families a decent standard of living". It is immediately clear that the authors of the Charter had no intention to introduce a precise common standard. Rather, the gauge of fairness is the extent to which the wage can afford workers and their families a decent standard of living. Assessment is therefore relative: the value of a given wage in relation to typical wage values, and the standard of living possible with such a wage, relative to normal living standards in each society. In its first conclusion on this provision, the Committee commented that the needs which wages should meet comprise not just the essential requisites of food, clothing and shelter but also more advanced and complex needs in the educational, cultural and social fields.[1] Again, different societies will have their own views on what constitute the main elements of a decent standard of living. Nevertheless, as the process of supervision requires clear methodology, the Committee decided to apply what became known as the 68% rule.

---

[1] Conclusions I, p, 26.

A. The 68 % rule

153. This rule was devised on the basis of expert studies carried out by the Council of Europe and the OECD.[1] It established a decency threshold at 68 % of average national earnings. Wages which fell beneath this threshold would not be in keeping with the principle of Article 4 para. 1. In order to accommodate the particular social and fiscal arrangements of states, the Committee would also consider the effect of various social, family and educational benefits and/or favourable taxation measures before deciding whether the obligation of the state had been fulfilled. Since the text of the provision itself refers to families, account was taken of the situation of a number of different single-wage household models: a single worker with no dependants, a single worker with two children, and a worker with dependent spouse and two children. This method proved difficult to apply for lack of adequate statistical data, and perhaps strayed away from the central notion of a fair wage to consider the full range of social and fiscal benefits for those in receipt of low pay. Following a period of reflection,[2] during which time it refrained from reaching conclusions under this provision, the Committee adopted a new approach to this provision which it used for the first time in Conclusions XIV-2.

B. A new approach

a. A new threshold

154. In the General Introduction to Conclusions XIV-2, the Committee describes the manner in which it arrived at its new method, which stipulates a new decency threshold calculated as 60 % of average national wages. It is important to note that net values are used, ie. after tax and social security deductions, whereas the Committee previously concentrated on gross figures. The change in method does not imply a change in interpretation. The Committee takes care to state that lowest wages should not fall too far below average wages, the notion underpinning its

---

[1] Conclusions V, pp. 25-26.

[2] See the Committee's announcement in Conclusions XIII-3, pp. 215-218.

previous approach. By concentrating on two key figures, the difficulties encountered in the past with obtaining data may be avoided. Improved sources of information exist at international level, notably Eurostat and the OECD. While states should still furnish the Committee with the required statistics, these other sources will be very useful in confirming or completing the information supplied by governments.

155. Two reasons are advanced for adjusting the assessment method. Firstly, the European Committee of Social Rights takes the view that changes in the earnings pattern of families since the Charter was drafted have been so substantial that it is no longer reasonable to expect that a single wage will meet all of a family's needs. The massive entry of women into the labour market over the past three decades renders the implicit assumption in the text of the Charter that there will be just one (male) wage-earner in every household erroneous. Reference is made to the Community Charter of the Fundamental Social Rights of Workers, 1989, which describes a fair wage as one which enables the individual worker to have a decent standard of living. It could also be argued that whereas in previous decades wage rates often included a family-related component (eg. married man's allowance or head of household payment), these payments are much rarer now. Any income supplements in respect of dependants now almost always come from the state in the form of social security, leaving the wage as, quite simply, the rate for the job.

156. The second reason is the need to be able to assess implementation of Article 4 para. 1 in a growing number of states, especially states from central and eastern Europe, the great majority of which are preparing to ratify the Charter. These states have quite different wage patterns and experience greater wage dispersion. The old 68 % rule was devised at a time when there were just 11 Contracting States which formed a relatively homogeneous economic group.[1] The new method is intended to apply sensibly and fairly to all states that have accepted Article 4 para. 1, whatever their stage of economic development and whatever the salient features of their wage structures.

---

[1] This was part of the rationale for the method. See Conclusions V, p. 26.

b.   Other considerations

157.   The 60 % rule is not the sole and conclusive consideration. It is the first step in the assessment of national compliance with Article 4 para. 1. Therefore, even if a wage is calculated as being above this threshold, it must also be sufficient in real terms to afford a decent standard of living. In other words, it must be clearly above the poverty line for that country. This is in fact a necessary clarification in the wider context of social justice enshrined in the Charter. In particular, the distinction must be drawn with the right to social assistance under Article 13. Under this provision, every individual without resources is entitled to adequate assistance. In other words, it is the duty of the state to provide whatever assistance is necessary for such persons to stay above the poverty line. A wage that fails to lift a person much further than that is not a fair wage. It is this essential difference which leads the Committee to state that the existence of a minimum income guarantee such as exists in most states is not directly relevant to the assessment of compliance under Article 4 para. 1.

158.   Where wages are found to fall under the 60 % threshold, the Committee will not automatically conclude that the situation violates the Charter. Instead, the state concerned will be requested to provide any additional information illustrating that the pay in question is nevertheless capable of purchasing a decent standard of living for the worker. Examples of relevant factors given by the Committee are health care, transport and education costs. However, where pay rates exist which result in a net remuneration of less than half of the net national average wage, the situation will be immediately held to be in violation of the Charter.

159.   Unlike the previous assessment method, social transfers will no longer be taken into account systematically, unless directly linked to the wage. Through its concentration on net wages, the assessment method already takes account of the impact of taxes and contributions on average and lowest wages. However, the Committee has decided that it will still consider the impact of any benefits on those in receipt of low pay. Arguably, by indicating its willingness to still consider, where appropriate, certain social transfers, the Committee is respecting the flexibility as to the means chosen which the final unnumbered paragraph of Article 4 permits. In states which have a statutory minimum wage, its net value will be used as the basis for the Committee's inquiry. Other-

wise, the Committee will seek information on the lowest rates of pay which actually exist, whether collectively agreed or simply a reflection of labour market tendencies. Also relevant is the number of workers in receipt of such wages. Comparisons are based on full-time rates.

160.   The term "remuneration" is to be interpreted as referring to all payments, in cash or in kind, recurrent or not (bonuses, premiums) which the worker receives in consideration for his labour.

161.   In introducing its new methodology, the Committee ends by emphasising the importance of Article 4 para. 1 within the group of rights protected by the Charter. It considers that this provision should form part of the hard core and urges wider acceptance of it. With a view to better supervision of the implementation of this provision, the Committee declares itself willing to meet with governmental representatives, a practice which is expressly contemplated under the Turin Protocol[1] and which has already occurred on a number of occasions.

c.   The new method applied

162.   The publication of the new method after the submission of national reports on the implementation of Article 4 para. 1 of the Charter meant that in most cases the Committee deferred its assessment for lack of reliable information on net average wages and net minimum wages.

163.   The Committee was able to conclude definitely in a number of cases however. Thus, it held that the situation in Malta was satisfactory. Unlike most other states, where accurate information on tax and social security deductions was lacking, the situation in Malta is clearer. According to the report, the national minimum wage on 1 January 1998 was 45.63 Maltese pounds (MTL). Although this data did not relate to the reference period, the Committee nevertheless considered it was in possession of sufficient information to assess the situation. It appears to have been persuaded in particular by the fact that income tax in Malta is payable

---

[1] Article 2 of the Protocol amending the European Social Charter proposes a new Article 24 for the latter, the third paragraph of which relates to direct contacts with governments and meetings, where necessary.

only on a significantly higher income: 57.69 MTL per week (single rate) or 76.92 MTL (married rate). Also, certain flat-rate payments increase the value of the minimum wage by 9 %. The Committee was able to accept that the 60 % threshold was clearly exceeded, even if there remained a question about the impact of social security deductions, estimated in previous Maltese reports to be approximately 1/12th of gross income. Other questions about the position of part-time workers and family workers were posed, to ensure that all workers enjoy the protection of this provision.

164.   The Committee found that the situations in Ireland, the Netherlands, Spain and the United Kingdom were not in conformity with the Charter.

165.   In relation to the situation in Ireland, the Committee had the advantage of a detailed report on the issue of low pay in Ireland[1] which provided it with sufficient information on the number of workers in receipt of *gross* wages which were less than 2.50 Irish punts (IEP), ie. practically half of the *net* average wage as calculated by Eurostat (4.94 IEP). 6.5 % of the workforce fell into this category – approximately 65,000 workers. Since the net income of this group could be expected to decrease somewhat after social security deductions, the Committee concluded that the evidence before it was sufficient to sustain a finding that the Charter had not been implemented properly, there being too great a gap between the wages of this group and average pay rates.

166.   The problem encountered in the Netherlands concerned young workers, that is between the ages of 15 and 23 years. The Committee was able to calculate that the net minimum wage during the reference period was equal to approximately 57 % of the net average wage. However, young workers may be paid at lower rates, decreasing from 85 % of the minimum wage at 22 years to 35 % at 15 years. On this basis, the Committee estimated that a worker aged 20 who was employed on the minimum wage would have a net salary of just 35 % of net average earnings. It may be noted that this particular feature of the Dutch labour market

---

[1] Report of the National Minimum Wage Commission.

has lead to a negative conclusion under this provision on several occasions in the past.[1]

167.   The situation in Spain was the subject of criticism on the part of the General Union of Workers (UGT), which claimed that there had been a steady decline in the relative value of the minimum wage over many years. Although the report did not supply net figures, it revealed that the gross minimum wage (paid fourteen times per year) amounted to just 39 % of the gross national average wage, as calculated by the government. Turning to Eurostat data, the Committee was able to compare the gross minimum wage for 1996 with the net average wage in the same year for a single worker (manual/non-manual) in the manufacturing sector, arriving at a value of 45 %. Given that the net minimum wage would be somewhat lower, the Committee decided that the situation was not in conformity with the Charter.

168.   Finally, as regards the situation in the United Kingdom, the Committee took note of the gross and net values of the national average wage. The relative value of a gross wage equal to half of the gross national average scarcely improved when considered net (rising to just 53 %, according to national data). Coupled with this, the Committee observed that a large group of workers (lowest paid decile) earned less than 40 % of the gross national wage. As with Ireland and Spain, the Committee considered that it had sufficient elements before it to conclude that the net wages of the lowest paid group lagged too far behind the national average to be compatible with the Charter.

169.   As for the other national situations examined, the Committee posed other questions on other points, such as the number of workers in receipt of the minimum wage, the position of workers not covered by collective agreements and, in cases where the situation appears to be unfavourable (eg. Greece, Iceland), how minimum wages can secure a decent standard of living when they apparently lag so far behind average earnings.

170.   In view of the large number of deferred conclusions, it is premature to try to assess the efficacy of the new methodology under Article 4 para. 1. The Committee's desire to simplify national

---

[1] Continuously from the ninth to thirteenth supervision cycles.

governments' task in assembling data on net income will hopefully bear fruit at the next occasion on which this provision comes before the Committee (2002). The disappointment which might be felt at the high number of deferrals during XIV-2 will hopefully be offset by clear and concise reporting, allowing this provision, which is one of the highlights of the Charter, to be fully applied.

II. Guarantees of remuneration

A. *The right to increased remuneration for overtime work*

171. Leading on from the guarantee of decent pay under the first paragraph of Article 4, the second paragraph requires states "to recognise the right of workers to an increased rate of remuneration for overtime work, subject to exceptions in particular cases". This is subject to exceptions in particular cases.

172. The approach of the Committee to this provision has been straightforward since the beginning, when it observed that the premise of this right is that the additional effort required by overtime should attract a higher rate of pay.[1]

a. Personal scope

173. This principle should apply generally across national labour markets. While the text of the provision itself contemplates exceptions, the Committee has emphasised often that this is not comparable to the type of situation permitted by Article 33 of the Charter.[2] Rather, the exceptions permitted in the present context must be limited and justified. The issue of justified exceptions has arisen on a number of occasions, in response to particular national situations:

---

[1] Conclusions I, p. 28, Conclusions XIV-2, p.35.

[2] Provisions to which Article 33 applies are considered to be complied with if the great majority of workers are protected, that is 80%. See United Kingdom XIV-2, p. 772.

– In the case of the Netherlands, the Committee accepted that those in receipt of high salaries could be denied the right to increased pay for overtime, on the basis that they were already sufficiently rewarded by their salary package. In the same vein, the example of *management executives* is commonly cited by the Committee as a group which may be excluded from overtime pay arrangements.

– Another group cited is *state employees*, although this should be understood as referring to senior civil servants and not the entire public sector. Confirmation of this is to be found in the most recent conclusion for Luxembourg, where the Committee concluded that the situation violated the Charter on the ground that not all overtime work performed by civil servants and public sector employees attracts a higher rate of pay.

174. Implementation of this provision is normally achieved through legislation or collective agreements, or both. The Committee pays close attention to the personal scope of all implementing measures and seeks information on the position of workers who appear to be without protection.[1] Until it is assured that the situation in practice is satisfactory, the Committee defers its assessment, repeatedly if necessary.[2] In the early cycles, the position of workers in agriculture was investigated systematically. In the most recent conclusions under this provision, the Committee had cause to seek further explanation of national case law in Luxembourg which reportedly denied higher overtime rates to agricultural workers.[3] Similarly, the arrangements covering domestic employees are often raised, leading on one occasion to a negative conclusion for Portugal.[4] where this group was found to be without protection. Subsequently, the Portuguese authorities submitted additional information on compensatory rest periods for domestic

---

[1] Denmark, IX-1 (coverage of collective agreements) Norway, XIV-2 (groups outside general legislation).

[2] This was the case with the United Kingdom in the twelfth and thirteenth supervision cycles, and is currently the case with Finland, even after three reports.

[3] Conclusions XIV-2, p. 479.

[4] Conclusions XIII-5, p. 167.

workers, allowing the Committee to revise its conclusion.[1] In relation to the United Kingdom, the application of this right to homeworkers has been raised. The information submitted by the British government suggests that this is not a widespread feature of this type of work.[2] The Committee did not pursue the matter further.

b. Implementation of the right

175. As mentioned at the beginning of this chapter, the final unnumbered paragraph of Article 4 envisages implementation of the various rights through different means which may be appropriate to national conditions. It is therefore acceptable in principle to argue that the right may be observed through custom and practice in the labour market. Nevertheless, as is clear from the United Kingdom's record of compliance with this provision, convincing evidence must be brought of the universal nature of such practice. Thus, although the Committee initially accepted that the right to increased pay for overtime working was respected in practice in the British labour market,[3] it subsequently revised its position.[4] It recalled that even if the Charter permits a certain margin of appreciation as to the means employed to implement Article 4, the result must be satisfactory. Although the British Government referred to a *"very widely held expectation that time worked in excess of normal basic hours will be paid at an enhanced rate"*, the Committee expressed its concern that almost one quarter of the workforce was not guaranteed increased remuneration for overtime through either collective agreement or statutory regulation. Subsequent British reports sought to convince the Committee on the basis of surveys and studies that this right is respected, but without success. After postponing assessment on a number of occasions pending production of convincing evidence, the Committee finally decided that the prolonged absence of clear indicators that workers did in practice enjoy this right justified its finding that the situa-

---

[1] Conclusions XIV-2, p. 646.

[2] *ibid.*, pp. 772-773.

[3] Conclusions IX-1, p. 41.

[4] Conclusions XII-1, pp. 95-96.

tion infringed the Charter.[1] It further voiced its concern at the lack of guarantees for workers. This case law suggests that a regulatory framework, whether statutory or collectively agreed, is an essential requirement in compliance with this provision of the Charter, since custom and practice do not readily lend themselves to verification.

176. Overtime pay rates commonly observed in states vary considerably. Statutory rates are often further increased by collective agreements.[2] The Charter does not offer any guidance as to the magnitude of the increase which should be paid. The Committee has concluded that the situation in Luxembourg is not satisfactory since civil servants and public sector employees are not entitled to increased pay unless the overtime work is performed between 10 pm and 6 am, at the weekend or on a public holiday.[3] A restriction of this nature is incompatible with the Charter. Recent legislative changes in Spain have lead the Committee to revise its previously favourable conclusion, since the relevant statutory provisions[4] no longer ensure a higher rate of remuneration for overtime work. Instead, the text merely provides that the rate cannot be less than the usual pay rate. In addition, the question of the overtime pay rate may be addressed through the employment contract alone, a factor which the Committee criticised as further weakening the position of the individual worker.[5]

177. Although the text of the provision refers to remuneration, the Committee considers that arrangements whereby overtime work is compensated with extra time off for the worker are not incompatible with the Charter. In such cases, the amount of time granted must correspond to an increased rate of remuneration, ie. it must be greater than the duration of the overtime performed. The Committee considered that Belgium failed to satisfy this provision

---

[1] Conclusions XIV-2, p. 772.

[2] For example, in Conclusions XIV-2 the increases observed range from 6.8% in the Belgian public service to 250% in certain collective agreements in Portugal for work at weekends or on public holidays.

[3] Conclusions XIV-2, p. 479.

[4] Section 35 of the Workers' Statute.

[5] Conclusions XIV-2, p. 682.

because public servants are not granted a longer rest period in consideration for overtime performed.[1] It has also raised this issue with Luxembourg.[2] The involvement of trade unions in determining whether overtime work should give rise to payment or time off appears to be relevant, although not imperative.[3]

c. Consequences of flexible working time

178. The issue of flexible working time has a direct bearing on the implementation of this provision. Under Article 2 paras. 1 and 5, the Committee investigated new statutory or collectively-agreed arrangements in detail during supervision cycle XIV-2. Arrangements which are based on the notion of average working time, calculated over a given period – normally less than one year – clearly challenge the traditional conception of overtime, since a longer working week is offset by a shorter week at a future date. Exceeding the average daily or weekly time is not, therefore, overtime and does not confer entitlement to increased remuneration. The Committee has declared that such arrangements are not incompatible with this provision, subject to closer scrutiny of the precise modalities in each case.[4] The notion of overtime continues to exist, however, even in the context of flexible working arrangements, to cover situations in which work is done beyond the limits laid down by the relevant legislation or collective agreement.[5] The ability of the Charter to adapt to new phenomena in the labour regulation and practice is well shown in the Committee's approach.

---

[1] *ibid.*, p. 134.

[2] *ibid.*, p. 479.

[3] *ibid.*, Finland, p. 228; France, p. 272.

[4] *ibid.*, p. 35. The situation in most states was considered to be in conformity with the Charter.

[5] *ibid.*, Austria, p. 89.

B.   The right to equal pay for work of equal value

179.   Under Article 4 para. 3, states undertake "to recognise the right of men and women workers to equal pay for work of equal value"

180.   The case law of the Committee on this provision has recently been described in detail in the monograph entitled *Equality between women and men in the European Social Charter*.[1] Readers are referred to this publication. A short summary of the case law under Article 4 para. 3 follows.

181.   States are required to ensure that this guarantee is legally enforceable under national law, which should accurately and unambiguously incorporate the concept.[2] It is permissible for the matter to be regulated by collective agreement, but unless it can be shown that all workers are covered, general legislation will be necessary, to ensure that the right applies to each and every employment relationship.

182.   The right to equal pay applies to all elements of the pay package, ie. all remuneration, in whatever form, which the employee receives from the employer as a consequence of the employment relationship.

183.   National law must provide for the nullity of employment contracts or collective agreements which offend against the principle of equal pay. A court or other appropriate authority must have the competence to waive the application of any such provisions. In the interests of effective application of the principle of equal pay, more radical remedies are advisable, such as the introduction of a statutory legal provision rendering any such stipulation null and void, the possibility for a court to declare this nullity by a decision applicable *erga omnes*, the introduction of a specific right for trade unions to take legal action in these matters, including the right to act as an intervener in individual litigation, or the possibility of class action on

---

[1] Social Charter Monographs – No. 2 (new edition).

[2] For example, Conclusions XIV-2, Turkey, p. 741.

the part of persons in whose interest it would be to have this nullity declared.[1]

184. Workers who invoke their right to equal pay must be legally protected from all forms of retaliation by the employer. In particular, dismissal on this ground must be prohibited. Where a worker is the victim of retaliatory action, there must be an adequate remedy which will both compensate the worker and serve as a deterrent to the employer. In cases of dismissal, the usual remedy should be reinstatement. Exceptionally, compensation may be admitted in cases where reinstatement is not possible or not desired by the worker.[2]

185. National law should not unduly restrict the scope for job comparisons, eg. by confining them to the same enterprise.[3]

186. In addition to verifying compliance with the formal legal requirements of Article 4 para. 3, the Committee also reviews wage data supplied by states on average differences in male and female earnings for various sectors of the economy. In this way, it is able to monitor developments within states from cycle to cycle.

C. *The right to reasonable notice of termination of employment*

a. The Committee's approach when assessing conformity

187. Under Article 4 para. 4, states undertake to recognise the right of all workers to a reasonable period of notice for termination of employment.

188. This paragraph may appear at first glance to have little to do with the protection of wages, but the purpose of notice is to ensure that between the decision to terminate the employment contract and its implementation, the worker concerned continues to earn a wage or, as is commonly possible, receives a payment equal to the remuneration which would have been due for the notice period.

---

[1]. For example, *ibid.*, Norway, p. 593.

[2]. For example, *ibid.*, Iceland, p. 374.

[3] Conclusions XIII-1, p. 121.

This paragraph is the least accepted provision of Article 4 (fifteen states out of twenty-two).

189.   Like the first paragraph of Article 4, this provision requires the Committee to exercise judgement in supervising compliance, assessing whether the notice periods provided for within a given state are reasonable. However, whereas the Committee has adopted a method to help form its judgement with respect to fair remuneration, its approach under this provision eschews any absolute definition of reasonableness, concentrating instead on particular situations which it concludes are unreasonable[1] within the meaning of the Charter. According to its case law, the Committee is guided by considerations of fairness, such as length of service in the firm, and the progressive character of the Charter. This was most recently recalled in Conclusions XIV-2 where the Committee reassessed the situation in France. Although this country had been considered to be in conformity with this paragraph for some time, the Committee stated that such conclusions were not immune to re-examination, given the progressive nature of the Charter. The notice period of two months stipulated in the Labour Code was accordingly found to be insufficient for workers with longer periods of service, the Committee stating that the prevailing employment situation in a state is relevant in determining whether the periods of notice granted to workers are reasonable.[2]

190.   The reference to the employment situation as a relevant consideration may be seen as a development in the Committee's reasoning under this provision, which mainly focuses on length of service, as do most national rules on this topic. Although there is no absolute definition of reasonableness under the Charter, the case law under this provision nevertheless gives a fairly clear idea

---

[1] Conclusions I, p. 29 and IV, p. 35.

[2] The conclusion in this instance is unsurprising, since the previous French report was submitted for cycle XIII-1. In the intervening time, the Committee examined reports from Belgium and Portugal and decided that the same notice period could not be accepted as reasonable for workers with long periods of service.

of the limits of unreasonableness.[1] In supervising compliance, the Committee examines a variety of sources: general legislation, specific employment regulations (eg. for civil servants), collective agreements and, subject to proof, custom.[2] In its most recent review of the implementation of this paragraph, the periods of notice observed ranged from two days for certain workers in Italy with less than two years' service to six months' notice in Sweden for workers with more than ten years' service. The former period was criticised, the latter was deemed acceptable.

b.   "Unreasonable" notice periods

191.   In several states, the first statutory notice period is one week.[3] The Committee has taken the view that for workers in the first six months of their employment, such a period is not reasonable[4] for the purpose of the Charter. The same conclusion was reached for Malta, where this is the minimum notice period for workers in their first year of service, Ireland, where this is the notice period for workers with between thirteen weeks and two years' service, and the United Kingdom, where it applies from after the first month to the end of the second year of service. The Committee has stated that workers with more than one year's service should receive at least one month's notice,[5] which helps to clarify the issue. However, there is as yet no case law on the minimum length of service which may be required before any notice period applies. Trial periods are a common feature in states, during which time the contract may be terminated with no notice. The issue has only arisen in relation to Portugal, with the Commit-

---

[1] A useful overview of its case law in this field has been published by the Committee: Fifth report on certain provisions of the Charter which have not been accepted, Council of Europe 1997.

[2] Conclusions VIII, United Kingdom, p. 74. The Committee did not find the desired level of proof in subsequent reports and therefore the conclusion remained negative.

[3] For example, Ireland, Malta, United Kingdom.

[4] Conclusions XIII-3, p. 267.

[5] Conclusions XIV-2, Spain, p. 684.

tee reserving its position until a more systematic review of national arrangements is possible.[1]

192.   A notice period of one month would seem to be acceptable for workers with up to five years' service. Thus the United Kingdom has been found to violate this provision by providing for just one week of notice per year of service during the first three years. Four and five weeks' notice in the fourth and fifth years are, however, compatible with the Charter.[2] After five years, the standard of protection required increases. Therefore, the four weeks' notice available in Ireland to workers with between five and ten years' service is unreasonable[3]. Similarly, the 28 days' notice granted to manual workers in Belgium with up to 20 years' service is not acceptable[4] (in respect of workers with more than five years' service). On the other hand, the arrangements in the United Kingdom for workers with more than five years' service (one extra week of notice per year of service up to a maximum of twelve weeks) have not attracted criticism.

193.   In a number of cases, the Committee has criticised a maximum limit of two months' notice: Belgium (56 days for manual workers with more than 20 years' service), France,[5] Ireland (8 weeks for workers with 15 years' service or more), Malta (8 weeks after 5 years' service). In each case, the Committee speaks of "longer periods of service". The conclusions reached for these countries suggests that this means twenty years or more, although in the Irish example the period of service at issue is fifteen years. Portugal was criticised in the past for a period of sixty days' notice in the case of workers with many years' service in the firm.[6] The subsequent report indicated that in addition to this, workers also received an indemnity of one month's pay per year of service, with a minimum payment equal to three months' wages. Since pay-

---

[1] Conclusions XIV-2, p. 648.

[2] *ibid.*, p. 773.

[3] *ibid.*, pp. 397-398.

[4] *ibid.*, p. 138.

[5] cf. paragraph 189 and second footnote.

[6] Conclusions XIII-3, p. 267.

ments of this nature may partially or totally replace the notice period, the situation was deemed acceptable.[1] As noted above, a maximum statutory period of twelve weeks notice appears to be reasonable in all cases, although, as the Committee recalls, it reserves the right to reassess national situations from cycle to cycle.[2]

194. Cases have arisen of notice periods which are linked not just to length of service but also to age. In Sweden, the Committee has found fault with the situation of workers in the painting and metal trades, since the applicable collective agreements provide for a single period of notice of one month until the age of thirty years.[3] The Swedish authorities have advanced a number of justifications for this arrangement. It was argued that the intention of the social partners was to reserve more favourable conditions for older workers who might have greater difficulty in finding new employment. Although it thought this motive reasonable, the Committee did not accept that it should eliminate the criterion of length of service.[4] It was also argued that few workers in the group concerned would have long periods of service by the age of thirty. The Committee replied that one month's notice would be insufficient after five years' service (which would not be difficult to achieve by that age). Other arguments that the trade unions had accepted the arrangement in return for better employment security and that the "last in first out" rule offered additional protection were not accepted. However, the Committee did accept that in principle national law may permit collective agreements to derogate from statutory minima if these are already reasonable in themselves and the reduced periods are not themselves unreasonable.[5]

---

[1] Conclusions XIII-5, pp. 169-170.

[2] Conclusions XIV-2, p. 774.

[3] See also the Netherlands, where the Civil Code lays down a period of notice of just one week where the worker is a minor, a situation criticised by the Committee.

[4] Conclusions XII-1, p. 106.

[5] See also Conclusions XIV-2, Norway, p. 594.

c.   General application of the right

195.   The right to a reasonable period of notice must be generally applied. Therefore the Committee ensures that all groups enjoy this protection. The fact that certain groups may have more favourable treatment (eg. be covered by more generous terms in a collective agreement) does not pose a problem, since the only obligation on states is to ensure that no worker is left without reasonable notice of termination of employment.[1] The application of this provision to workers on fixed-term contracts has been commented on by the Committee in various contexts. In relation to Portugal, the Committee observed that national law lays down different notice periods (seven, thirty or sixty days) for workers with fixed-term contracts, but only where the term of the contract is contingent on an event which will occur at an unspecified future date, eg. where the worker is temporarily replacing another worker on sick leave whose date of return is not yet determined. This situation was considered acceptable. In respect to Spain, the Committee concluded that the situation was not compatible with this provision since workers with fixed-tem contracts concluded for a period of more than one year are entitled to just fifteen days' notice. In the case of a fixed-term contract, the concept of notice remains pertinent with reference not to the term, which is usually known since the start, but to premature termination. Since fixed-term contracts may last several years, such workers merit the same level of protection as those with more permanent employment. Other groups to which the Committee's attention has been drawn are childminders, seafarers, homeworkers and persons in atypical work.[2]

196.   The Appendix to the Charter states that Article 4 para. 4 shall be so understood as not to prohibit immediate dismissal for any serious offence. The Committee examines the instances in which national law permits dismissal without notice so as ensure that they do not go beyond this exception.[3]

---

[1] Conclusions XIII-4, p. 352.

[2] See for example Conclusions XIV-2, France, p. 275.

[3] Conclusions XIV-2, p. 513.

197.　This provision applies not just to dismissal, but to all cases of termination of employment. In the case of Spain, the Committee has criticised the provision of the Workers' Statute which lays down a flat-rate indemnity of one month's pay where employment is terminated in the death, retirement or incapacity of the employer, without any additional provision for workers with longer service records.[1]

198.　Occasionally, states have argued that formal notice periods laid down in national law or in collective agreements are effectively extended by various procedural arrangements which have the effect of delaying the final decision to dismiss (eg. the duty on employers in the Netherlands to seek the authorisation of the labour administration before dismissing a worker,[2] the obligation of Swedish employers to consult with trade unions before dismissing a worker[3], the granting of fourteen days to Irish civil servants to make representations against a proposed dismissal.[4] To date, these arguments have not been accepted, since these procedures all operate prior to the decision to terminate employment, ie. before the period of notice begins to run.

199.　Since the purpose of the notice period is to allow workers seek new employment, the Committee takes note of arrangements made to permit the worker time off for this purpose[5].

D.　Limitation of deductions from wages

200.　Under Article 4 para. 5, states undertake to "permit deductions from wages only under conditions and to the extent prescribed by national laws or regulations or fixed by collective agreements or arbitration awards".

---

[1] *ibid.*, p. 684.

[2] Conclusions IX-1, p. 45.

[3] Conclusions XI-1, p. 75.

[4] Conclusions XIV-2, p. 398.

[5] Conclusions XIII-1, p. 124.

201.   Unlike the preceding paragraphs, the personal scope of this provision is qualified by the Appendix, under which states may be considered to comply with this provision if it is applied to the great majority of workers, the exceptions being those not so covered. This qualification has not deterred the Committee from investigating the extent to which this right is secured throughout the labour market.[1]

202.   The text of this paragraph is more precise as to the means to be employed in securing the right than the other provisions of Article 4, since only national laws or regulations, or collective agreements, or arbitration awards are acceptable. It is not surprising therefore that the Committee is unconvinced by generalised statements concerning labour market practice and wage deductions.[2]

203.   The underlying principle of this provision is that the worker's wage should be subject to deductions only in circumstances which are well-defined in a legal instrument (covering the basis and procedure) and subject to the limits specified therein.

a.   Conditions governing wage deductions

204.   As regards the conditions under which deductions may be made, the Committee fully investigates national arrangements. In countries where the applicable rules are complex, this can lead to repeated deferrals until the Committee is satisfied that the right is properly implemented.[3] If there appears to be insufficient precision, the situation may be considered unsatisfactory. An example of this is Italy, where the Committee has repeatedly rejected arguments put forward by the Italian authorities that Article 36 of the Constitution alone, which entitles workers to remuneration *"proportional to the quality and quantity of the work performed, and at all events sufficing to guarantee a free and decent life for the worker and his family"* effectively implements Article 4 para. 5 of the Charter with

---

[1] See for example Conclusions XIV-2, Turkey, p. 743.

[2] Conclusions III, p. 29.

[3] For example, Luxembourg, Addendum to Conclusions XIII-5 and Conclusions XIV-2.

respect to wage deductions arising from debts owed to the employer by the worker. Were the Italian Government to produce national case law illustrating how this operates in practice, there could be grounds for reassessing the situation, since the Committee has considered the approach of the courts on this issue in other countries.[1]

205.   National legislation which appears to permit the parties to the employment contract the scope to agree on deductions invariably attracts closer scrutiny. In its most recent supervision of this provision, the Committee raised questions with Ireland, Norway and the United Kingdom over the possibility of deductions being permitted with the written consent of the worker, as laid down in the relevant national regulations. It is submitted that this degree of latitude is not compatible with the Charter. Similarly, the Committee investigates the legal basis for fines on workers, which, being deductions, must conform to the standard stipulated in this provision. In the case of Malta, for example, the Committee was satisfied that the Director of Labour could supervise the imposition of fines under an employment contract.[2] In contrast, the Committee has asked Luxembourg how many workers could have be subject to fines under the rules of the workplace, as drawn up by the employer alone, since such deductions would not be compatible with the Charter unless the great majority of workers were not affected.[3]

206.   When considering the conditions under which deductions may be made to wages, the Committee looks not just to the situations in which this arises (typically repayment of advances, fines and compensation for damage caused by the worker), but also to the procedures involved. It takes note of any duty to consult worker representatives, the right of the worker to make his case, and seeks information on appeal to the courts.[4] This is quite in keeping with the principle behind this provision, ie. that deductions to

---

[1] For example, Greece, Conclusions XIII-1, p. 127 and Turkey, (see para. 208 and second footnote).

[2] Conclusions XIII-2, p. 267.

[3] Conclusions XIV-2, p. 482.

[4] For example, Conclusions XIII-1, Norway, p. 128, and Turkey, p. 227.

wages should only be permissible in accordance with a higher legal norm than the employment contract.

b.   Limitations to wage deductions

207.   At the same time, the Committee considers the limits laid down in national law for wage deductions. In doing so, it examines rules relating to, *inter alia,* attachments, garnishee orders and maintenance payments. National rules on this point vary, choosing either to protect a fraction of the wage from deductions (three quarters in Turkey, four fifths in Belgium, five sixths in Portugal), or stipulating a minimum sum which must be set aside for the worker (as in Finland and Malta). In assessing these limits, the Committee's concern is that the worker be assured of an income which assures subsistence for them and their dependants.[1] Where this information is missing, the Committee insists on receiving it with the next report.[2] It also keeps limits under review, to ensure that they remain reasonable. In this context, it observed that the limit laid down in Malta of 100 Maltese pounds (MLT) had not been revised since Malta's first report and hoped that this would be done before the next report in 2002.[3]

208.   On the issue of limits to deductions, the Committee has often considered the effect of maintenance payments on the wage, as these are not always subject to the same limitations as other deductions.[4] It therefore seeks detailed information on the criteria adopted by the courts in such cases so as to ensure that the worker retains a sufficient income.[5]

209. The foregoing overview of the case law under Article 4 of the Charter indicates the determination of the Committee to keep both formal and practical implementation of this provision under close review. While the quality of national reports is not always such as to facilitate this task, the collective complaints procedure may

---

[1] Conclusions XI-1, p. 76.

[2] See conclusions for Ireland and the United Kingdom in Conclusions XIV-2.

[3] Conclusions XIV-2, p. 514.

[4] As in Malta, for example.

[5] For example, Conclusions XIII-1, Turkey, p. 270.

present the Committee in the future with the opportunity to examine national situations in more depth and with the benefit of an adversarial procedure. It is surely likely that on the sensitive and crucial issue of wage protection, there will be no shortage of complaints.

Conclusion

The Council of Europe fully endorses the view that social rights are human rights, to be protected and promoted with the same energy as the provisions of the European Convention on Human Rights.

This survey of the provisions and case law of the European Social Charter on conditions of employment has made clear that basic social rights are justiciable, and lend themselves to international supervision. The entry into force of the Collective Complaints Protocol in 1998 should enhance this aspect of the Charter by allowing the European Committee of Social Rights to investigate national situations in greater detail, and with the benefit of an adversarial procedure. In particular, since the reporting period for Articles 2, 3 and 4 is four years, the Collective Complaints Protocol will permit trade unions or international non-governmental organisations to focus attention on any serious problems which may arise in the intervening period.

The nature of employment in Europe is undergoing enormous change, driven by a variety of factors, not least the pressure of competition from other continents. States have reacted by introducing substantial reforms in their employment legislation, and further changes may be expected in time. In this changing context, the principles enshrined in the Charter must be kept clearly in view. The revised Charter introduces significant reforms in this area, improving on annual leave entitlement, offering protection to those engaged in night work, involving social partners in the formulation of health and safety policy for work places and promoting preventive and advisory occupational health services. These improvements indicate that far from being called into question, basic labour rights will remain a prominent feature of employment in Europe. It is to be hoped that the Contracting Parties to the Charter will proceed rapidly to ratification of the revised Charter, permitting the new standards to be applied throughout Europe.

Appendix I

Extracts from the European Social Charter and the Additional Protocol

A. Social Charter of 18 October 1961[1]

Part I[2]

The Contracting Parties accept as the aim of their policy, to be pursued by all appropriate means, both national and international in character, the attainment of conditions in which the following rights and principles may be effectively realised:

...

2. All workers have the right to just conditions of work.

3. All workers have the right to safe and healthy working conditions.

4. All workers have the right to a fair remuneration sufficient for a decent standard of living for them-selves and their families.

...

---

[1] The principal provisions examined in this monograph are: Articles 2 paras. 1 to 5, 3 paras. 1 to 3 and 4 paras. 1 to 5.

[2] Part I of the Charter lists the rights and principles that states recognise as the aim of their policies and Part II covers the various rights under a corresponding number of articles, dividing them into one or more binding obligations. Part I is a political statement, whereas the articles and paragraphs of Part II are obligations, but the terms of the paragraphs in Part I allow an interpretation of the corresponding articles of Part II to be made.

Part II

The Contracting Parties undertake, as provided for in Part III,[1] to consider themselves bound by the obligations laid down in the following articles and paragraphs.

Article 2 – The right to just conditions of work

With a view to ensuring the effective exercise of the right to just conditions of work, the Contracting Parties undertake:

1.[2]   to provide for reasonable daily and weekly working hours, the working week to be progressively reduced to the extent that the increase of productivity and other relevant factors permit;

2.[3]   to provide for public holidays with pay;

3.[4]   to provide for a minimum of two weeks annual holiday with pay;

4.[5]   to provide for additional paid holidays or reduced working hours for workers engaged in dangerous or unhealthy occupations as prescribed;

5.[1]   to ensure a weekly rest period which shall, as far as possible, coincide with the day recognised by tradition or custom in the country or region concerned as a day of rest.

---

[1] See below the relevant extracts from Part III.

[2] Article 2 para. 1 has been accepted by all the states having ratified the European Social Charter (see above, third footnote to the overview) except Austria, Denmark, Turkey and the United Kingdom.

[3] Article 2 para. 2 has been accepted by all the states having ratified the European Social Charter (see above, third footnote to the overview) except Cyprus, Iceland, Poland and Turkey.

[4] Article 2 para. 3 has been accepted by all the states having ratified the European Social Charter (see above, third footnote to the overview) except Turkey.

[5] Article 2 para. 4 has been accepted by all the states having ratified the European Social Charter (see above, third footnote to the overview) except Cyprus, Denmark, Iceland, Malta and Turkey.

Article 3 – The right to safe and healthy working conditions

With a view to ensuring the effective exercise of the right to safe and healthy working conditions, the Contracting Parties undertake:

1.[2]   to issue safety and health regulations;

2.[3]   to provide for the enforcement of such regulations by measures of supervision;

3.[4]   to consult, as appropriate, employers' and workers' organisations on measures intended to improve industrial safety and health.

Article 4 – The right to a fair remuneration

With a view to ensuring the effective exercise of the right to a fair remuneration, the Contracting Parties undertake:

1.[5]   to recognise the right of workers to a remuneration such as will give them and their families a decent standard of living;

2.[1]   to recognise the right of workers to an increased rate of remuneration for overtime work, subject to exceptions in particular cases;

---

[1] Article 2 para. 5 has been accepted by all the states having ratified the European Social Charter (see above, third footnote to the overview) except Turkey.

[2] Article 3 para. 1 has been accepted by all the states having ratified the European Social Charter (see above, third footnote to the overview) except Finland and Turkey.

[3] Article 3 para. 2 has been accepted by all the states having ratified the European Social Charter (see above, third footnote to the overview) except Denmark, Finland and Turkey.

[4] Article 3 para. 3 has been accepted by all the states having ratified the European Social Charter (see above, third footnote to the overview) except Turkey.

[5] Article 4 para. 1 has been accepted by all the states having ratified the European Social Charter (see above, third footnote to the overview) except Cyprus, the Czech Republic, Denmark, Finland, Hungary, Poland and Turkey.

3.[2]   to recognise the right of men and women workers to equal pay for work of equal value;

4.[3]   to recognise the right of all workers to a reasonable period of notice for termination of employment;

5.[4]   to permit deductions from wages only under conditions and to the extent prescribed by national laws or regulations or fixed by collective agreements or arbitration awards.

The exercise of these rights shall be achieved by freely concluded collective agreements, by statutory wage-fixing machinery, or by other means appropriate to national conditions.

Appendix to Article 4 para. 4

This provision shall be so understood as not to prohibit immediate dismissal for any serious offence.

Appendix to Article 4 para. 5

It is understood that a Contracting Party may give the undertaking required in this paragraph if the great majority of workers are not permitted to suffer deductions from wages either by law or through collective agreements or arbitration awards, the exceptions being those persons not so covered.

---

[1] Article 4 para. 2 has been accepted by all the states having ratified the European Social Charter (see above, third footnote to the overview) except Cyprus, Hungary and Turkey.

[2] Article 4 para. 3 has been accepted by all the states having ratified the European Social Charter (see above, third footnote to the overview) except Cyprus, Hungary, Ireland and the United Kingdom.

[3] Article 4 para. 4 has been accepted by all the states having ratified the European Social Charter (see above, third footnote to the overview) except Austria, Cyprus, Denmark, Finland, Germany, Hungary, Luxembourg and Turkey.

[4] Article 4 para. 5 has been accepted by all the states having ratified the European Social Charter (see above, third footnote to the overview) except Cyprus, Denmark and Hungary.

Part III

Article 20 – Undertakings

1. Each of the Contracting Parties undertakes:

(a) to consider Part I of this Charter as a declaration of the aims which it will pursue by all appropriate means, as stated in the introductory paragraph of that part;

(b) to consider itself bound by at least five of the following articles of Part II of this Charter: Articles 1, 5, 6, 12, 13, 16 and 19;

(c) in addition to the articles selected by it in accordance with the preceding sub-paragraph, to consider itself bound by such a number of articles or numbered paragraphs of Part II of the Charter as it may select, provided that the total number of articles or numbered paragraphs by which it is bound is not less than 10 articles or 45 numbered paragraphs.

...

3. Any Contracting Party may, at a later date, declare by notification to the Secretary General that it considers itself bound by any articles or any numbered paragraphs of Part II of the Charter which it has not already accepted under the terms of paragraph 1 of this article. Such undertakings subsequently given shall be deemed to be an integral part of the ratification or approval, and shall have the same effect as from the thirtieth day after the date of the notification.

...

Part V

Article 33 – Implementation by collective agreements

1. In member States where the provisions of paragraphs 1, 2, 3, 4 and 5 of Article 2, paragraphs 4, 6 and 7 of Article 7 and paragraphs 1, 2, 3 and 4 of Article 10 of Part II of this Charter are matters normally left to agreements between employers or employers' organisations and workers' organisations, or are normally carried out otherwise than by law, the undertakings of those paragraphs may be given and compliance with them shall be

treated as effective if their provisions are applied through such agreements or other means to the great majority of the workers concerned.

2. In member States where these provisions are normally the subject of legislation, the undertakings concerned may likewise be given, and compliance with them shall be regarded as effective if the provisions are applied by law to the great majority of the workers concerned.

Appendix to the Social Charter

Scope of the Charter in terms of persons protected:

1. Without prejudice to Article 12, paragraph 4, and Article 13, paragraph 4, the persons covered by Articles 1 to 17 include foreigners only insofar as they are nationals of other Contracting Parties lawfully resident or working regularly within the territory of the Contracting Party concerned, subject to the understanding that these articles are to be interpreted in the light of the provisions of Articles 18 and 19.

This interpretation would not prejudice the extension of similar facilities to other persons by any of the Contracting Parties.

B.   Additional protocol of 5 May 1988[1]

Part I

The Parties accept as the aim of their policy to be pursued by all appropriate means, both national and international in character, the attainment of conditions in which the following rights and principles may be effectively realised:

---

[1] The Protocol has been ratified by: Denmark, Finland, Greece, the Netherlands, Norway and Slovakia.

Article 3 – Right to take part in the determination and improvement of the working conditions and working environment

1.   With a view to ensuring the effective exercise of the right of workers to take part in the determination and improvement of the working conditions and working environment in the undertaking, the Parties undertake to adopt or encourage measures enabling workers or their representatives, in accordance with national legislation and practice, to contribute:

> a.   to the determination and the improvement of the working conditions, work organisation and working environment;
>
> b.   to the protection of health and safety within the undertaking;
>
> ...
>
> d.   to the supervision of the observance of regulations on these matters.

2.   The Parties may exclude from the field of application of paragraph 1 of this Article, those undertakings employing less than a certain number of workers to be determined by national legislation or practice.

Article 7 – Implementation of the undertakings given

1.   The relevant provisions of Articles 1 to 4 of Part II of this Protocol may be implemented by:

> a.   laws or regulations;
>
> b.   agreements between employers or employers' organisations and workers' organisations;
>
> c.   a combination of those two methods; or
>
> d.   other appropriate means.

2.   Compliance with the undertakings deriving from Articles 2 and 3 of Part II of this Protocol shall be regarded as effective if the provisions are applied, in accordance with paragraph 1 of this Article, to the great majority of the workers concerned.

Appendix to the Protocol

Articles 2 and 3

1.   For the purpose of the application of these articles, the term "workers' representatives" means persons who are recognised as such under national legislation or practice.

2.   The term "national legislation and practice" embraces as the case may be, in addition to laws and regulations, collective agreements, other agreements between employers and workers' representatives, customs, as well as relevant case law.

3.   For the purpose of the application of these articles, the term "undertaking" is understood as referring to a set of tangible and intangible components, with or without legal personality, formed to produce or provide services for financial gain and with power to determine its own market policy.

4.   It is understood that religious communities and their institutions may be excluded from the application of these articles, even if these institutions are "undertakings" within the meaning of paragraph 3 Establishments pursuing activities which are inspired by certain ideals or guided by certain moral concepts, ideals and concepts which are protected by national legislation, may be excluded from the application of these articles to such an extent as is necessary to protect the orientation of the undertaking.

5.   It is understood that where in a State the rights set out in Articles 2 and 3 are exercised in the various establishments of the undertaking, the Party concerned is to be considered as fulfilling the obligations deriving from these provisions.

Article 3

This provision affects neither the powers and obligations of States as regards the adoption of health and safety regulations for workplaces, nor the powers and responsibilities of the bodies in charge of monitoring their application.

...

Appendix II

Extracts from the explanatory report to the Additional Protocol of 1988

Articles 2 and 3

Article 2, paragraph 1

37. The term "undertaking" is defined in the appendix. It should be noted that, although the undertaking should have the power to make decisions regarding its market policy, it is not essential for workers to be informed at the place at which the undertaking's management makes such decisions. On the contrary, this provision allows the Parties complete discretion to fix, or to leave management and labour to determine freely, the various levels of information and consultation, which need not coincide with the decision-making level. In the case of, for instance, decentralised undertakings, information and consultation should in any event, to be effective, occur in the various production units if they are also practised at the decision-making centres. See also the comment in the appendix about the "establishments of the undertaking".

38. With regard to multinational undertakings, the definition of the term "undertaking" shall be understood to apply to each production unit enjoying decision-making powers and located in the territory of a Party.

39. Sub-paragraph a of this paragraph stipulates that only information about the economic and financial situation of the undertaking must be communicated (subject to the proviso about secrecy and confidentiality). Other information, for example about industrial property or manufacturing or trade secrets, need not be disclosed.

40. This restriction supplements the general restriction which may be applied to the exercise of the rights set forth in this Protocol pursuant to Article 31 of the Charter, to which Article 8 of the Protocol refers.

41.   It goes without saying that under this provision the possibility of refusing to disclose certain information or of requiring confidentiality may naturally be included not only in legislation or regulations but also in collective agreements or other agreements between employers and workers' representatives.

42.   The expression "and in a comprehensible way" in sub-paragraph a has been inserted following a proposal by the Assembly in Opinion No. 131, which considered it useful to describe more precisely the kind of information to be disclosed.

43.   In order to be effective, "consultation" in the relevant fields should be preceded by the furnishing of appropriate "information": the scope of consultation is thus coterminous with that of the information provision, the only restrictions being those provided in sub-paragraph b, emphasised by the use of the co-ordinating conjunction "and" at the end of sub-paragraph a.

Article 2, paragraph 2

44.   This paragraph makes it possible for the Parties to apply the provisions on information and consultation of workers only to undertakings employing more than a certain number of workers. This option was included because it appeared that for reasons of efficiency and having regard also to the special circumstances associated with the size of certain undertakings, the establishment of specific information and consultation structures was, in many countries, envisaged or required only when the number of employees exceeded a certain minimum. The establishment of such structures is generally not obligatory in undertakings employing fewer workers than the number stipulated in legislation, regulations or agreements in force between the Parties. Moreover, in small undertakings, information and consultation processes often exist in fact and operate readily, making the introduction of rigid and sometimes complex procedures unnecessary.

45.   The Parties have accordingly been given the option of providing for the creation of information and consultation structures or systems only when the number of employees exceeds a certain level. If this option is exercised, the threshold (or thresholds) will need to be indicated in the reports to be submitted under Article 6. In the case of undertakings with fewer employees than the thresholds(s), the Parties will not, on the other hand, be required to

explain information and consultation procedures but may communicate such information thereon as is in their possession.

46.   It should further be noted that only the criterion of the undertaking's size (number of employees) is mentioned in this article, as other criteria relating to the undertaking's nature or activities may be covered by the appendix to the Protocol (Articles 2 and 3, paragraph 4), and/or by Article 31 of the Charter, to which Article 8 of the Protocol refers. The possibility that undertakings may also be excluded because collective agreements or other agreements applying to them contain no provisions relating to information or consultation is, on the other hand, covered by Article 7 of the Protocol. In this case, however, the workers not afforded this right must be a minority or, more exactly, those enjoying the right to be informed and consulted must constitute the great majority of the workers concerned in the country in question.

Article 3, paragraph 1

47.   The matters listed in this article are frequently covered by collective agreements or other agreements between employers and workers' representatives.

48.   Sub-paragraph c comes from a proposal of the Assembly (see Opinion No. 131) and, for a better understanding of the text, a certain number of the services and facilities thus referred to have been listed in the appendix.

49.   This article in no way prejudices the right to bargain collectively provided for in Article 6 of the Charter, as is clear from Article 8 of the Protocol.

50.   The expression "to take part in" covers all situations in which workers or their representatives are in any way whatsoever associated with the procedures for making decisions or taking certain measures, without, however, enjoying a right of joint decision-making or of veto over decisions still the responsibility of the head of the undertaking.

51.   The contribution to the "supervision of the observance" of health and safety regulations is to be effected pursuant to the rules in force in each country and without prejudice to the jurisdiction and responsibilities of the bodies and authorities vested with the necessary powers. The role of workers or their representatives is

not to replace the bodies responsible for this supervision but rather to ensure that supervision is as effective as possible.

Article 3, paragraph 2

52. The earlier comments on the analogous provision in Article 2 also apply here.

...

68. Under the heading "Articles 2 and 3", paragraph 4 of the appendix has been inserted, *inter alia*, to meet the situation in the Federal Republic of Germany where certain categories of undertakings with an "orientation" (*Tendenzbetriebe*) are excluded from the scope of the 1972 Act on the Organisation of Undertakings or from certain of its provisions. These are "companies and establishments that directly and predominantly:

1. pursue political, coalition, religious, charitable, educational, scientific or artistic objects; or

2. serve purposes of publishing or expressing opinions covered by the second sentence of section 5 (1) of the Basic Law (Constitution)."

69. Under the heading "Articles 2 and 3", paragraph 5 of the appendix refers to "establishments of the undertaking". In fact an undertaking may consist of one or more production units economically and legally bound to a single management centre. Such production units then constitute as many component establishments of the undertaking, and it is understood that where within a state rights Nos. 2 and 3 are effectively exercised within the various establishments of the undertaking in question, the Party concerned shall be deemed to fulfil its obligations under these provisions.

Appendix III

Extracts from the Forms for Reports

A. **European Social Charter** (articles 2, 3 and 4) – revised Form for Reports adopted by the Committee of Ministers in November 1999.

Article 2 para. 1

A.   Please indicate what statutory provisions apply in respect of the number of working hours, daily and weekly and the duration of the daily rest period.

B.   Please indicate what rules concerning normal working hours and overtime are usual in collective agreements, and what is the scope of these rules.

C.   Please indicate the average working hours in practice for each major professional category.

D.   Please indicate to what extent working hours have been reduced by legislation, by collective agreements or in practice during the reference period and, in particular, as a result of increased productivity.

E.   Please describe, where appropriate, any measures permitting derogations from legislation in your country regarding daily and weekly working hours and the duration of the daily rest period (see also Article 2 paras. 2, 3 and 5).

Please indicate the reference period to which such measures may be applied.

Please indicate whether any such measures are implemented by legislation or by collective agreement and in the latter case, at what level these agreements are concluded and whether only representative trade unions are entitled to conduct negotiations in this respect.

F.   If some workers are not covered by provisions of this nature, whether contained in legislation, collective agreements or other measures, please state what proportion of all workers is not so covered (see Article 33 of the Charter).

Article 2 para. 2

A.   Please indicate the number of public holidays with pay laid down by legislation, stipulated by collective agreement or established by practice during the last calendar year.

B.   Please indicate what rules apply to public holidays with pay according to legislation, collective agreements or practice.

Please describe, where appropriate, whether measures permitting derogation from legislation in your country regarding daily and weekly working hours have an impact on rules pertaining to public holidays with pay.

C.   If some workers are not covered by provisions of this nature, whether contained in legislation, collective agreements, or other measures, please state what proportion of all workers is not so covered (see Article 33 of the Charter).

Article 2 para. 3

A.   Please indicate the length of annual holidays under legislative provisions or collective agreements; please also indicate the minimum period of employment entitling workers to annual holidays.

Please describe, where appropriate, whether measures permitting derogation from statutory rules in your country regarding daily and weekly working hours have an impact on rules pertaining to the duration of annual holidays.

B.   Please indicate the effect of incapacity for work through illness or injury during all or part of annual holiday on the entitlement to annual holidays.

C.   Please indicate if it is possible for workers to renounce their annual holiday.

D.   Please indicate the customary practice where legislation or collective agreements do not apply.

E.   If some workers are not covered by provisions of this nature, whether contained in legislation, collective agreements or other measures, please state what proportion of all workers is not covered (see Article 33 of the Charter).

Article 2 para. 4

A.   Please state the occupations regarded as dangerous or unhealthy. If a list exists of these occupations, please supply it.

B.   Please state what provisions apply under legislation or collective agreements or otherwise in practice as regards reduced working hours or additional paid holidays in relation to this provision.

C.   If some workers are not covered by provisions of this nature, whether contained in legislation, collective agreements or other measures, please state what proportion of all workers concerned is not covered (see Article 33 of the Charter).

Article 2 para. 5

A.   Please indicate what provisions apply according to legislation, collective agreements or otherwise in practice as regards weekly rest periods.

Please indicate whether postponement of the weekly rest period is provided for these provisions and, if so, please indicate under what circumstances and over what period of reference.

Please indicate, where appropriate, whether measures derogating from statutory rules in your country regarding daily and weekly working time have an impact on rules relating to the weekly rest period.

B.   Please indicate what measures have been taken to ensure that workers obtain their weekly rest period in accordance with this paragraph.

C.   If some workers are not covered by provisions of this nature, whether contained in legislation, collective agreements or other measures, please state what proportion of all workers is not covered (see Article 33 of the Charter).

Please indicate, for Article 2 as a whole, the rules applying to workers in atypical employment relationships (fixed-term contracts, part-time, replacements, temporaries, etc.).

Article 3 para. 1

A.   Please list the principal legislative or administrative provisions issued in order to protect the physical and mental health and the safety of workers, indicating clearly:

    a.   their material scope of application (risks covered and the preventive and protective measures provided for), and

    b.   their personal scope of application (whatever their legal status – employees or not – and whatever their sector of activity, including home workers and domestic staff).

Please specify the rules adopted to ensure that workers under atypical employment contracts enjoy the same level of protection as other workers in an enterprise.

B.   Please indicate the special measures taken to protect the health and safety of workers engaged in dangerous or unhealthy work.

Article 3 para. 2

A.   Please indicate the methods applied by the Labour Inspection to enforce health and safety regulations and please also give information, *inter alia*, statistical, on:

    a.   the places of work, including the home, subjected to the control of the Labour Inspection, indicating the categories of enterprises exempted from this control;

    b.   the number of control visits carried out;

    c.   the proportion of workers covered by these visits.

B.   Please describe the system of civil and penal sanctions guaranteeing the application of health and safety regulations and also provide information on violations committed:

    a.   the number of violations;

    b.   the sectors in which they have been identified;

    c.   the action, including judicial, taken in this respect.

C.   Please provide statistical information on occupational accidents, including fatal accidents, and on occupational diseases by sectors of activity specifying what proportion of the labour force is covered by the statistics. Please describe also the preventive measures taken in each sector.

Article 3 para. 3

Please indicate if consultations with workers' and employers' organisations are provided for in this connection by law, if they take place in practice and at what level (national, regional, at the sectoral or enterprise level).

Article 4 para. 1

A.   Please state what methods are provided and what measures are taken to provide workers with a fair wage, having regard to national living standards and particularly to the changes in the cost of living index and in national income.

B.   Please specify if these include methods for fixing minimum wage standards by law or collective agreements.

C.   Please indicate what proportion of wage-earners are without protection in respect of wages, either by law or collective agreement.

D.   Please provide information on:

—   national net average wage (.ie. after deduction of social security contributions and taxes);

—   national net minimum wage if applicable or the net lowest wages actually paid (i.e. after deduction of social security contributions and taxes).

Please provide information, where possible, on:

—   the proportion of workers receiving the minimum wage or the lowest wage actually paid (after deduction of social security contributions and taxes);

—   the trend in the level of the minimum net wage and/or the lowest wage actually paid compared to national net average wage and any available studies on this subject.

Article 4 para. 2

A.   Please mention what provisions apply according to legislation and collective agreements as regards overtime pay, the method used to calculate the increased rates of remuneration and the categories of work and workers to which they apply.

Please specify what provisions apply in respect of overtime pay on Saturdays, Sundays and other special days or hours (including night work).

B.   Please mention any special cases for which exceptions are made.

Please indicate, where appropriate, whether measures permitting derogation from legislation in your country regarding daily and weekly working hours (see Article 2 para. 1) have an impact on remuneration or compensation of overtime.

Article 4 para. 3

A.   Please indicate how the principle of equal pay for work of equal value is applied; state whether the principle applies to all workers.[1]

B.   Please indicate the progress which has been made in applying this principle.

C.   Please describe the protection afforded to workers against retaliatory measures, including dismissal.

Please indicate the procedures applied to implement this protection.

Article 4 para. 4

A.   Please indicate if periods of notice are provided for by legislation, by collective agreements or by practice and if so, indicate the length of such periods, notably in relation to seniority in the enterprise.

Please indicate whether the periods of notice established by legislation can be derogated by collective agreements.

Please indicate the periods of notice applicable to part-time workers and to home workers.

---

[1] The term "equal pay for work of equal value" in this Form is to be understood in terms of ILO Convention No. 100 (Equal Remuneration), Article 1.

Please indicate in which cases a worker may not be given a notice period.

Please indicate whether provision is made for notice periods in the case of fixed-term contracts which are not renewed.

B.   Please indicate whether wage-earners may challenge the legality of such notice of termination of employment before a judicial authority.

Article 4 para. 5

A.   Please describe how and to what extent observance of this paragraph is ensured in your country, specifying the ways in which this right is exercised, both as regards deductions made by the employer for his own benefit and for the benefit of third parties.

Please indicate whether legislation, regulations or collective agreements provide for the non-seizability of a part of the wage.

B.   Please state whether the measures described are applicable to all categories of wage-earners. If this is not the case, please give an estimate of the proportion of workers not covered and, if appropriate, give details of the categories concerned.

B.   **Additional Protocol** (article 3) – Form for Reports adopted by the Committee of Ministers in May 1991

Article 3

A.   Please state if workers participate directly or through their representatives in the determination and improvement of the working conditions and the working environment and, in the latter case, how such representatives are appointed at the various levels (workshop, establishment, undertaking, etc.).

B.   Please give general description of the structures, procedures and arrangements for workers to take part in determining the work conditions in undertakings in general and, when appropriate, in the various activity sectors of undertakings. This information should be specified according to each of the various areas referred to in paragraph 1 of Article 3 of the Protocol. If appropriate, please describe at what levels within the undertaking these rights are exercised and describe how.

C.   Please state if workers' participation concerns all of the areas covered by Article 3, paragraph 1, of the Protocol.

D.   Please state the number or numbers of workers below which undertakings are not required to make provision for the participation of workers in the determination of their working conditions.

E.   If some workers are not covered by provisions of this type prescribed by legislation, collective agreements or other measures, please state the proportion of workers not so covered (see Article 7 of the Protocol and the relevant provision in the Appendix).

F.   Please state whether undertakings other than those specified in paragraph 2 of Article 3 are excluded from the application of this provision in the meaning of the Appendix to the Protocol (Articles 2 and 3, paragraph 4) and indicate their nature and the sector of activity involved.

C.   Revised Charter (articles 2, 3, 4 and 22) – Form for Reports to be adopted by the Committee of Ministers in December 2000.

Article 2 paras. 1 to 7

Please indicate, for Article 2 as a whole, the rules applying to workers in atypical employment relationships (fixed-term contracts, part-time, replacements, temporaries, etc.).

Article 2 para. 1

A.   Please indicate what statutory provisions apply in respect of the number of working hours, daily and weekly and the duration of the daily rest period.

B.   Please indicate what rules concerning normal working hours and overtime are usual in collective agreements, and what is the scope of these rules.

C.   Please indicate the average working hours in practice for each major professional category.

D.   Please indicate to what extent working hours have been reduced by legislation, by collective agreements, or in practice during the reference period and, in particular, as a result of increased productivity.

E.   Please describe, where appropriate, any measures permitting derogations from legislation in your country regarding daily and weekly working hours and the duration of the daily rest period (see also Article 2 paras. 2, 3 and 5).

Please indicate the reference period to which such measures may be applied.

Please indicate whether any such measures are implemented by legislation or by collective agreement and in the latter case, at what level these agreements are concluded and whether only representative trade unions are entitled to conduct negotiations in this respect.

F.   If some workers are not covered by provisions of this nature, whether contained in legislation, collective agreements or other measures, please state what proportion of all workers is not so covered (see Article I of the revised Social Charter).

Article 2 para. 2

A.   Please indicate the number of public holidays with pay laid down by legislation, stipulated by collective agreement or established by practice during the last calendar year.

B.   Please indicate what rules apply to public holidays with pay according to legislation, collective agreements or practice.

Please describe, where appropriate, whether measures permitting derogation from legislation in your country regarding daily and weekly working hours have an impact on rules pertaining to public holidays with pay.

C.   If some workers are not covered by provisions of this nature, whether contained in legislation, collective agreements, or other measures, please state what proportion of all workers is not so covered (see Article I of the revised Social Charter).

Article 2 para. 3

A.   Please indicate the length of annual holidays under legislative provisions or collective agreements; please also indicate the minimum period of employment entitling workers to annual holidays.

Please describe, where appropriate, whether measures permitting derogation from statutory rules in your country regarding daily and weekly working hours have an impact on rules pertaining to the duration of annual holidays.

B.   Please indicate the effect of incapacity for work through illness or injury during all or part of annual holiday on the entitlement to annual holidays.

C.   Please indicate if it is possible for workers to renounce their annual holiday.

D.   Please indicate the customary practice where legislation or collective agreements do not apply.

E.   If some workers are not covered by provisions of this nature, whether contained in legislation, collective agreements or other measures, please state what proportion of all workers is not covered (see Article I of the revised Social Charter).

Article 2 para. 4

A.   Please indicate the policies and the legislative measures taken to eliminate or to reduce the inherent risks of dangerous or unhealthy occupations. Please also describe the procedures for periodic review and evaluation.

B.   Please state the occupations regarded as dangerous or unhealthy. If a list exists of these occupations, please supply it.

C.   Where it has not yet been possible to eliminate or reduce sufficiently these risks, please state what provisions apply under legislation or collective agreements or otherwise in practice as regards reduced working hours or additional paid holidays in relation to this provision of the revised Charter.

D.   If some workers are not covered by provisions of this nature, whether contained in legislation, collective agreements or other measures, please state what proportion of all workers con

Article 2 para. 5

A.   Please indicate what provisions apply according to legislation, collective agreements or otherwise in practice as regards weekly rest periods.

Please indicate whether postponement of the weekly rest period is provided for these provisions and, if so, please indicate under what circumstances and over what period of reference.

Please indicate, where appropriate, whether measures derogating from statutory rules in your country regarding daily and weekly working time have an impact on rules relating to the weekly rest period.

B.   Please indicate what measures have been taken to ensure that workers obtain their weekly rest period in accordance with this paragraph.

C.   If some workers are not covered by provisions of this nature, whether contained in legislation, collective agreements or other measures, please state what proportion of all workers is not covered (see Article I of the revised Social Charter).

Article 2 para. 6

A.   Please indicate the rules (in legislation, collective agreements) or other provisions which apply for informing workers in writing of the essential aspects of their contract or employment relationship.

Please describe the content and form of this information, as well as the point at which it must be communicated in writing.

Please indicate how rules or other measures are applied in practice.

B.   If the rules are not of a general nature (Appendix to the revised Social Charter), please indicate the exceptions and referring to item b of the Appendix, please state the reason for their exclusion (see Article I of the revised Social Charter).

Article 2 para. 7

A.   Please indicate the rules (legislation, collective agreements or in practice) in force which ensure that workers performing night work benefit from measures to take account of the special nature of the work (medical examinations, breaks, compensatory time off, access to company services, inspections, circumstances in which it is possible to transfer to day work, etc.). Please indicate in particular the hours to which the term "night work" applies.

B.   Please indicate the proportion of any workers who are not covered (see Article I of the revised Social Charter).

Article 3 paras. 1 to 4

Please indicate how organisations of employers and workers are consulted by the authorities on the measures required to implement each of the paragraphs of Article 3 (procedure and level of consultation, content and frequency of consultation).

Article 3 para. 1

Please describe policy in the field of occupational safety, occupational health and the working environment and the measures taken to improve occupational safety and health and to prevent health and safety risks. Please describe also the measures of implementation of this policy as well as procedures for its periodic review and evaluation.

Article 3 para. 2

A.   Please list the principal legislative or administrative provisions issued in order to protect the physical and mental health and safety of workers, indicating clearly:

    a.   their material scope of application (risks covered and the preventive and protective measure provided for) and;

    b.   their personal scope of application (whatever the legal status – employees or not – and whatever their sector of activity, including home workers and domestic staff).

Please specify the rules adopted to ensure that workers under atypical employment contracts enjoy the same level of protection as other workers in an enterprise.

B.   Please indicate the special measures taken to protect the health and safety of workers engaged in dangerous or unhealthy work.

Article 3 para. 3

A.   Please indicate the methods applied by the Labour Inspectorate to enforce health and safety regulations and please also give information, *inter alia*, statistical, on:

    a.   the places of work, including the home, subjected to the control of the Labour Inspection, indicating the categories of enterprises exempted from this control;

    b.   the number of control visits carried out;

    c.   the proportion of workers covered by these visits.

B.   Please describe the system of civil and penal sanctions guaranteeing the application of health and safety regulations and also provide information on violations committed:

    a.   the number of violations;

    b.   the sectors in which they have been identified;

    c.   the action, including judicial, taken in this respect.

C.   Please provide statistical information on occupational accidents, including fatal accidents, and on occupational diseases by sectors of activity specifying what proportion of the labour force is covered by the statistics. Please describe also the preventive measures taken in each sector.

Article 3 para. 4

A.   Please indicate whether occupational health services (health, security and occupational health services) exist in all companies and in all sectors. If not, please state whether plans have been made to establish them, when they will be implemented in practice and/or whether provision is made for inter-company services.

B.   Please describe the functions, organisation and operation of occupational health services.

Article 4 para. 1

A.   Please state what methods are provided and what measures are taken to provide workers with a fair wage, having regard to national living standards and particularly to the changes in the cost of living index and in national income.[1]

B.   Please specify if these include methods for fixing minimum wage standards by law or collective agreements.

---

[1] If your country has accepted Article 16, there is no need to give information here concerning family allowances, etc.

C.   Please indicate what proportion of wage-earners are without protection in respect of wages, either by law or collective agreement.

D.   Please provide information on:

–   national net average wage[1] (i.e. after deduction of social security contributions and taxes;)[2]

–   national net minimum wage if applicable or the net lowest wages actually paid (i.e. after deduction of social security contributions and taxes).[3]

Please provide information, where possible, on:

–   the proportion of workers receiving the minimum wage or the lowest wage actually paid (after deduction of social security contributions and taxes);

–   the trend in the level of the minimum net wage and/or the lowest wage actually paid compared to national net average wage and any available studies on this subject.

---

[1] In principle the net average wage should be the overall average for all sectors of economic activity. The average wage may be calculated on an annual, monthly, weekly, daily or hourly basis. Wages cover remuneration in cash paid directly and regularly by the employer at the time of each wage payment. This includes normal working hours, overtime and hours not worked but paid, when the pay for these latter are included in the returned earnings. Payments for leave, public holidays and other paid individual absences may be included insofar as the corresponding days or hours are also taken into account to calculate wages per unit of time.

[2] The net wage (average and minimum) should be calculated for the standard case of a single worker. Family allowances and social welfare benefits should not be taken into account. Social security contributions should be calculated on the basis of the employee contribution rates laid down by law or collective agreements etc. and withheld by the employer. Taxes are all taxes on earned income. They should be calculated on the assumption that gross earnings represent the only source of income and that there are no special grounds for tax relief other than those associated with the situation of a single worker receiving either the average wage or the minimum wage. Indirect taxes are thus not taken into account.

[3] The net minimum wage should be given in units of time comparable to those used for the average wage.

Article 4 para. 2

A.   Please mention what provisions apply according to legislation and collective agreements as regards overtime pay, the method used to calculate the increased rates of remuneration and the categories of work and workers to which they apply.

Please specify what provisions apply in respect of overtime pay on Saturdays, Sundays and other special days or hours (including night work).

B.   Please mention any special cases for which exceptions are made.

Please indicate, where appropriate, whether measures permitting derogation from legislation in your country regarding daily and weekly working hours (see Article 2 para. 1) have an impact on remuneration or compensation of overtime.

Article 4 para. 3

A.   Please indicate how the principle of equal pay for work of equal value is applied; state whether the principle applies to all workers.

B.   Please indicate the progress which has been made in applying this principle.

C.   Please describe the protection afforded to workers against retaliatory measures, including dismissal.

Please indicate the procedures applied to implement this protection.

Article 4 para. 4

A.   Please indicate if periods of notice are provided for by legislation, by collective agreements or by practice and if so, indicate the length of such periods, notably in relation to seniority in the enterprise.

Please indicate whether the periods of notice established by legislation can be derogated by collective agreements.

Please indicate the periods of notice applicable to part-time workers and to home workers.

Please indicate in which cases a worker may not be given a notice period.

Please indicate whether provision is made for notice periods in the case of fixed-term contracts which are not renewed.

B.   Please indicate whether wage-earners may challenge the legality of such notice of termination of employment before a judicial authority.

Article 4 para. 5

A.   Please describe how and to what extent observance of this paragraph is ensured in your country, specifying the ways in which this right is exercised, both as regards deductions made by the employer for his own benefit and for the benefit of third parties.

Please indicate whether legislation, regulations or collective agreements provide for the non-seizability of a part of the wage.

B.   Please state whether the measures described are applicable to all categories of wage-earners. If this is not the case, please give an estimate of the proportion of workers not covered and, if appropriate, give details of the categories concerned.

Article 22

A.   Please describe the rules and/or the mechanisms whereby the right of workers to information and consultation within the undertaking either directly or through their representatives is guaranteed, for example through legislation, collective agreements or other means.

Please indicate by whom and on what basis the workers' representatives are designated.

B.   Please state whether workers' participation concerns all of the areas covered by Article 22:

−   the determination and improvement of the working conditions, work organisation and working environment;

−   the protection of health and safety within the undertaking;

−   the organisation of social and socio-cultural services within the undertaking;

– the supervision of the observance of regulations on these matters.

C.   If some workers are not covered by provisions of this type either by legislation, collective agreements or other measures, please indicate the proportion of workers not so covered.

D.   Please indicate whether certain undertakings are excluded from the obligations contained in Article 22 on the grounds that they employ less than a certain number of workers. If so, please state the specified number of workers below which undertakings are not required to comply with these provisions.

E.   Please indicate whether there are certain undertakings, such as religious undertakings or other undertakings within the meaning of para. 4 of the appendix to Article 22, excluded from the rights guaranteed in this provision. If so please provide details on this subject.

F.   Please describe the legal remedies available to workers or their representatives who consider that their rights under this provision have not been respected. Please indicate the applicable sanctions.

Appendix IV

Extracts from the revised European Charter of 3 May 1996[1]

Part II

The Parties undertake, as provided for in Part III,[2] to consider themselves bound by the obligations laid down in the following articles and paragraphs.

Article 2 — The right to just conditions of work

With a view to ensuring the effective exercise of the right to just conditions of work, the Parties undertake:

1.[3]   to provide for reasonable daily and weekly working hours, the working week to be progressively reduced to the extent that the increase of productivity and other relevant factors permit;

2.[4]   to provide for public holidays with pay;

3.[1]   to provide for a minimum of four weeks' annual holiday with pay;

---

[1] Certain of the provisions of the revised Charter repeat those of the Charter or of the Additional Protocol referred to in this monograph without changes: these are Articles 2 paras. 1, 2 and 5 and 4 paras. 1 to 5 of the Charter, plus Article 3 of the Additional Protocol.

[2] See below the relevant extracts from Part III.

[3] Article 2 para. 1 has been accepted by all the states having ratified the revised European Social Charter (see above, third footnote to the overview) except Sweden.

[4] Article 2 para. 2 has been accepted by all the states having ratified the revised European Social Charter (see above, third footnote to the overview) except Sweden.

4.[2] to eliminate risks in inherently dangerous or unhealthy occupations, and where it has not yet been possible to eliminate or reduce sufficiently these risks, to provide for either a reduction of working hours or additional paid holidays for workers engaged in such occupations;

5.[3] to ensure a weekly rest period which shall, as far as possible, coincide with the day recognised by tradition or custom in the country or region concerned as a day of rest;

6.[4] to ensure that workers are informed in written form, as soon as possible, and in any event not later than two months after the date of commencing their employment, of the essential aspects of the contract or employment relationship;

7.[5] to ensure that workers performing night work benefit from measures which take account of the special nature of the work.

Article 3 — The right to safe and healthy working conditions

With a view to ensuring the effective exercise of the right to safe and healthy working conditions, the Parties undertake, in consultation with employers' and workers' organisations:

1.[6] to formulate, implement and periodically review a coherent national policy on occupational safety, occupational health and the

---

[1] Article 2 para. 3 has been accepted by all the states having ratified the revised European Social Charter (see above, third footnote to the overview) except Romania.

[2] Article 2 para. 4 has been accepted by all the states having ratified the revised European Social Charter (see above, third footnote to the overview) except Sweden.

[3] Article 2 para. 5 has been accepted by all the states having ratified the revised European Social Charter (see above, third footnote to the overview).

[4] Article 2 para. 6 has been accepted by all the states having ratified the revised European Social Charter (see above, third footnote to the overview).

[5] Article 2 para. 7 has been accepted by all the states having ratified the revised European Social Charter (see above, third footnote to the overview) except Sweden.

[6] Article 3 para. 1 has been accepted by all the states having ratified the revised European Social Charter (see above, third footnote to the overview).

working environment. The primary aim of this policy shall be to improve occupational safety and health and to prevent accidents and injury to health arising out of, linked with or occurring in the course of work, particularly by minimising the causes of hazards inherent in the working environment;

2.[1] to issue safety and health regulations;

3.[2] to provide for the enforcement of such regulations by measures of supervision;

4.[3] to promote the progressive development of occupational health services for all workers with essentially preventive and advisory functions.

Article 4 – The right to a fair remuneration

With a view to ensuring the effective exercise of the right to a fair remuneration, the Parties undertake:

1.[4] to recognise the right of workers to a remuneration such as will give them and their families a decent standard of living;

2.[5] to recognise the right of workers to an increased rate of remuneration for overtime work, subject to exceptions in particular cases;

3.[1] to recognise the right of men and women workers to equal pay for work of equal value;

---

[1] Article 3 para. 2 has been accepted by all the states having ratified the revised European Social Charter (see above, third footnote to the overview).

[2] Article 3 para. 3 has been accepted by all the states having ratified the revised European Social Charter (see above, third footnote to the overview).

[3] Article 3 para. 4 has been accepted by all the states having ratified the revised European Social Charter (see above, third footnote to the overview) except Romania and Sweden.

[4] Article 4 para. 1 has been accepted by all the states having ratified the revised European Social Charter (see above, third footnote to the overview).

[5] Article 4 para. 2 has been accepted by all the states having ratified the revised European Social Charter (see above, third footnote to the overview) except Sweden.

4.[2] to recognise the right of all workers to a reasonable period of notice for termination of employment;

5.[3] to permit deductions from wages only under conditions and to the extent prescribed by national laws or regulations or fixed by collective agreements or arbitration awards.

The exercise of these rights shall be achieved by freely concluded collective agreements, by statutory wage-fixing machinery, or by other means appropriate to national conditions.

...

Article 22 — The right to take part in the determination and improvement of the working conditions and working environment[4]

With a view to ensuring the effective exercise of the right of workers to take part in the determination and improvement of the working conditions and working environment in the undertaking, the Parties undertake to adopt or encourage measures enabling workers or their representatives, in accordance with national legislation and practice, to contribute:

    a.   to the determination and the improvement of the working conditions, work organisation and working environment;

    b.   to the protection of health and safety within the undertaking;

...

---

[1] Article 4 para. 3 has been accepted by all the states having ratified the revised European Social Charter (see above, third footnote to the overview).

[2] Article 4 para. 4 has been accepted by all the states having ratified the revised European Social Charter (see above, third footnote to the overview).

[3] Article 4 para. 5 has been accepted by all the states having ratified the revised European Social Charter (see above, third footnote to the overview) except Sweden.

[4] Article 22 has been accepted by all the states having ratified the revised European Social Charter (see above, third footnote to the overview) except Romania.

d.   to the supervision of the observance of regulations on these matters.

...[1]

Part III

Article A — Undertakings

1.   Subject to the provisions of Article B below, each of the Parties undertakes:

...

b.   to consider itself bound by at least six of the following nine articles of Part II of this Charter: Articles 1, 5, 6, 7, 12, 13, 16, 19 and 20;

c.   to consider itself bound by an additional number of articles or numbered paragraphs of Part II of the Charter which it may select, provided that the total number of articles or numbered paragraphs by which it is bound is not less than sixteen articles or sixty-three numbered paragraphs.

Part V

Article I — Implementation of the undertakings given

1.   Without prejudice to the methods of implementation foreseen in these articles the relevant provisions of Articles 1 to 31 of Part II of this Charter shall be implemented by:

a.   laws or regulations;

---

[1] The revised Charter has also introduced new rights concerning conditions of employment: the right to protection against dismissal (Article 24); the right of workers to the protection of their claims in the event of the insolvency of their employer (Article 25); the right of workers' representatives to protection in the undertaking and facilities to be accorded to them (Article 28) and the right to information and consultation in collective redundancy procedures (Article 29).

b. agreements between employers or employers' organisations and workers' organisations;

c. a combination of those two methods;

d. other appropriate means.

2. Compliance with the undertakings deriving from the provisions of paragraphs 1, 2, 3, 4, 5 and 7 of Article 2, paragraphs 4, 6 and 7 of Article 7, paragraphs 1, 2, 3 and 5 of Article 10 and Articles 21 and 22 of Part II of this Charter shall be regarded as effective if the provisions are applied, in accordance with paragraph 1 of this article, to the great majority of the workers concerned.

...

Appendix to the revised Social Charter

Article 2, paragraph 6

Parties may provide that this provision shall not apply:

a. to workers having a contract or employment relationship with a total duration not exceeding one month and/or with a working week not exceeding eight hours;

b. where the contract or employment relationship is of a casual and/or specific nature, provided, in these cases, that its non-application is justified by objective considerations.

Article 3, paragraph 4

It is understood that for the purposes of this provision the functions, organisation and conditions of operation of these services shall be determined by national laws or regulations, collective agreements or other means appropriate to national conditions.

Article 4, paragraph 4

This provision shall be so understood as not to prohibit immediate dismissal for any serious offence.

Article 4, paragraph 5

It is understood that a Party may give the undertaking required in this paragraph if the great majority of workers are not permitted to suffer deductions from wages either by law or through collective agreements or arbitration awards, the exceptions being those persons not so covered.

Articles 21 and 22

1.   For the purpose of the application of these articles, the term "workers' representatives" means persons who are recognised as such under national legislation or practice.

2.   The terms "national legislation and practice" embrace as the ase may be, in addition to laws and regulations, collective agreements, other agreements between employers and workers' representatives, customs as well as relevant case law.

3.   For the purpose of the application of these articles, the term "undertaking" is understood as referring to a set of tangible and intangible components, with or without legal personality, formed to produce goods or provide services for financial gain and with power to determine its own market policy.

4.   It is understood that religious communities and their institutions may be excluded from the application of these articles, even if these institutions are "undertakings" within the meaning of paragraph 3. Establishments pursuing activities which are inspired by certain ideals or guided by certain moral concepts, ideals and concepts which are protected by national legislation, may be excluded from the application of these articles to such an extent as is necessary to protect the orientation of the undertaking.

5.   It is understood that where in a state the rights set out in these articles are exercised in the various establishments of the undertaking, the Party concerned is to be considered as fulfilling the obligations deriving from these provisions.

6.   The Parties may exclude from the field of application of these articles, those undertakings employing less than a certain number of workers, to be determined by national legislation or practice.

Article 22

1. This provision affects neither the powers and obligations of states as regards the adoption of health and safety regulations for workplaces, nor the powers and responsibilities of the bodies in charge of monitoring their application.

2. The terms "social and socio-cultural services and facilities" are understood as referring to the social and/or cultural facilities for workers provided by some undertakings such as welfare assistance, sports fields, rooms for nursing mothers, libraries, children's holiday camps, etc.

Appendix V

Extracts from the explanatory report to the revised European Social Charter

Part II

...

Article 2 – The right to just conditions of work

21. Two paragraphs have been amended (paragraphs 3 and 4), the others remain unchanged:

Paragraph 3

22. This provision provides for an increase in annual holidays, from the two weeks provided by the Charter to four weeks.

Paragraph 4

23. This provision, which in the Charter provides for additional paid holidays or reduced working hours for workers engaged in dangerous or unhealthy occupations, has been amended so as to reflect present-day policies which aim to eliminate the risks to which workers are exposed. The idea is that additional paid holidays or reduced working hours should only be provided where it has not been possible to eliminate or reduce sufficiently the risks inherent in dangerous or unhealthy occupations. This provision should be seen as a complement to the revised Article 3, which emphasises the prevention of occupational accidents.

24. Two new paragraphs have been added:

Paragraph 6

25. The obligation on the Parties under this paragraph is to ensure that workers are informed about the essential aspects of their contract or employment relationship.

26.   The "essential aspects" of the contract or employment relationship of which workers shall be informed have not been specified in the provision. However, reference as to the minimum requirements in this respect may be found in European Community Directive (91/533) on an employer's obligation to inform employees of the conditions applicable to the contract or employment relationship (Article 2). In principle the provision covers all workers, but the appendix stipulates that two exceptions can be made, namely Parties may provide that the provisions shall not apply to workers whose contract of employment covers a very short period of time or whose contract or employment relationship is of a casual or of a specific nature provided it is justified by objective considerations.

Paragraph 7

27.   The general recognition of the fact that night work places special constraints on workers, both men and women led to the inclusion of this paragraph in the revised Charter. Furthermore, whereas Article 8, paragraph 4.a of the Charter provided that the employment of women workers in general for night work in industrial employment should be regulated, the corresponding provision in the revised Charter protects women only in the case of maternity. The other women previously protected by Article 8, paragraph 4.a of the Charter are therefore now covered by Article 2, paragraph 7 of the revised Charter on the same conditions as men, in conformity with the principle of equality. It should however be pointed out that the new provision does not require the existence of regulations.

28.   The provision contains no definition of night work, which is to be provided by national legislation or practice.

Article 3 – The right to safe and healthy working conditions

29.   This Article contains two new paragraphs (paragraphs 1 and 4) and two paragraphs (paragraphs 2 and 3) which, together with the new preamble of the Article correspond, respectively, to Article 3, paragraphs 1 and 3 of the Charter and to Article 3, paragraph 2 and 3 of the Charter.

30.   The requirement for consultation with employers' and workers' organisations which is contained in Article 3, paragraph 3 of the Charter has been included in the preamble of Article 3 of the

revised Charter and consequently applies to the four paragraphs contained in Article 3 of this instrument.

Paragraph 1

31.   This paragraph obliges the Parties to formulate, implement and periodically review a coherent national policy on occupational safety, occupational health and the working environment. It emphasises that the aim of this policy shall be to improve occupational safety and health and to prevent accidents and injury to health, *inter alia*, by minimising risks.

Paragraph 2

32.   This paragraph corresponds to Article 3, paragraphs 1 and 3 of the Charter.

Paragraph 3

33.   This paragraph corresponds to Article 3, paragraphs 2 and 3 of the Charter.

Paragraph 4

34.   This provision provides that the Parties shall promote the progressive development of occupational health services for all workers with essentially preventive and advisory functions.

35.   The terms "occupational health services" shall include the French concept of *médecine du travail*.

36.   In the appendix it is provided that for the purposes of this provision the function, organisation and conditions of operation of occupational health services shall be determined by national laws or regulations, collective agreements or other means appropriate to national conditions.

...

81.   Articles 20 to 23 correspond to the provisions of Articles 1 to 4 of the Additional Protocol of 1988. Paragraphs 2, 3 and 4 of Article 1, paragraph 2 of Article 2 and paragraph 2 of Article 3 have been moved to the appendix for the purposes of harmonisation. This change does not affect the nature and scope of the legal obligations accepted under these provisions.

82.   The explanatory report to the Additional Protocol of 1988 remains relevant.

Appendix VI

Supervisory machinery of the European Social Charter

A. System of supervision based on state reports[1]

System for the submission of reports:

Cycle XV

States concerned	Articles	Reference period	Date for submission of the report	Publication of Conclusions	Publication of Governmental Committee report	Committee of Ministers' decisions
All Contracting Parties XV-1	1. Hard core: Articles 1, 5, 6, 12, 13, 16 and 19 (except 1 para. 4)	1997-1998	30 June 1999	28 February 2000	October 2000	December 2000
All Contracting Parties XV-2	2. Half non-hard core: Articles 7, 8, 11, 14, 17 and 18 + 1 and 4 of the Additional Protocol	1995-1998	Either 30 June 1999 or 31 March 2000	31 December 2000	October 2001	December 2001

Cycle XVI

States concerned	Articles	Reference period	Date for submission of the report	Publication of Conclusions	Publication of Governmental Committee report	Committee of Ministers' decisions
All Contracting Parties XVI-1	1. Hard core	1999-2000	30 June 2001	28 February 2002	October 2002	December 2002
All Contracting Parties XVI-1	2. Half non-hard core: Articles 2, 3, 4, 9, 10 and 15 + 2 and 3 of the Additional Protocol	1997-2000	Either 30 June 2001 or 31 March 2002	31 December 2002	October 2003	December 2003

---

[1] See above, European Social Charter — an overview, for a reminder of the supervisory system based on reports by states.

European Social Charter

Supervisory mechanism

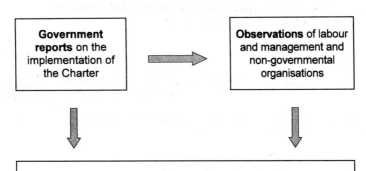

<table>
<tr><td>

Government reports on the implementation of the Charter

</td><td>

Observations of labour and management and non-governmental organisations

</td></tr>
</table>

EUROPEAN COMMITTEE OF SOCIAL RIGHTS

Assesses from a legal standpoint the compliance of national law and practice with the obligations arising from the Charter

GOVERNMENTAL COMMITTEE

Prepares the decisions of the Committee of Ministers: selects situations which should be the subject of recommendations

COMMITTEE OF MINISTERS

Adopts a resolution at the end of each supervision cycle

Where appropriate, Issues recommendations requesting states to bring national law and practice into conformity with the Charter

European Social Charter
Collective complaints procedure

International organisations of employers and trade unions (ETUC, UNICE, IOE)	Representative national organisations of employers and trade unions	International non-governmental organisations entered on a list drawn up by the Governmental Committee	Representative national non-governmental organisations competent in the matters covered by the Charter

(subject to a declaration by the state)

C O M P L A I N T S

EUROPEAN COMMITTEE OF SOCIAL RIGHTS

Decides on the admissibility of complaints

Draws up a report containing its conclusion as to whether or not the state concerned has violated the Charter

---

COMMITTEE OF MINISTERS

Adopts a resolution which closes the procedure and, where appropriate; issues a recommendation to the state concerned

GOVERNMENTAL COMMITTEE

In certain cases, may be consulted by the Committee of Ministers

Appendix VII

Major international norms relating to conditions of employment

I.   Worldwide norms

A.   *Norms of the United Nations Organisation*

1.   Universal Declaration of Human rights (1948)

–   entitlement of all to the realisation of the economic, social and cultural rights indispensable for dignity and the free development of personality (Article 22);

–   right to just and favourable conditions of work (Article 23 para. 1);

–   right to equal pay for equal work (Article 23 para. 2);

–   right to just and favourable remuneration ensuring everyone who works and their family an existence worthy of human dignity and supplemented, if necessary, by other means of social protection (Article 23 para. 3);

–   right to rest and leisure, including reasonable limitation of working hours and periodic holidays with pay (Article 24);

–   right of everyone to a standard of living adequate for the health and well-being of himself and of his family (Article 25 para. 1).

2.   International Covenant on Economic, Social and Cultural Rights (1966)

–   fair wages and equal remuneration for work of equal value without distinction of any kind, in particular between men and women (Article 7 para. a i.);

–   remuneration providing a decent living for workers and their families (Article 7 para. a ii.);

– safe and healthy working conditions (Article 7 para. b);

– rest, leisure and reasonable limitation of working hours and periodic holidays with pay, as well as remuneration for public holidays (Article 7 para. d);

– right of everyone to an adequate standard of living for himself and his family (Article 11).

3. *Convention on the Elimination of All Forms of Discrimination against Women*

– right to equal remuneration, including benefits, and to equal treatment in respect of work of equal value, as well as equality of treatment in the evaluation of the quality of work (Article 11, para. 1*d*.).

B.   Norms of the International Labour Organisation

1. *Working hours*

– Convention No. 1 on Hours of Work (Industry) (1919);

– Convention No. 30 on Hours of Work (Commerce and Offices) (1930);

– Convention No. 46 on Hours of Work (Coal Mines) (Revised, 1935);

– Convention No. 47 on a Forty-hour Week (1935);

– Convention No. 51 on the Reduction of Hours of Work (Glass-Bottle Works) (1935);

– Convention No. 61 on the Reduction of Hours of Work (Textiles) (1937);

– Convention No. 67 on Hours of Work and Rest Periods (Road Transport) (1939);

– Recommendation No. 116 on the Reduction of Hours of Work (1962);

– Convention No. 153 and Recommendation No. 161 on Hours of Work and rest periods (Road Transport) (1979);

– Convention No. 171 and Recommendation No. 178 on night work (1990);

– Convention No. 175 and Recommendation No. 182 on part-time work (1994).

2. *Weekly rest periods*

– Convention No. 14 on Weekly Rest (industry) (1921);

– Convention No. 106 and Recommendation No. 103 on Weekly Rest (Commerce and Offices) (1957).

3. *Paid holidays*

– Convention No. 52 and Recommendation No. 47 on Holidays with Pay (1936);

– Convention No. 101 and Recommendation No. 93 on Holidays with Pay (Agriculture) (1952);

– Convention No. 132 on Holidays with Pay (Revised), (1970).

4. *Health and safety at work*

– Recommendation No. 3 on prevention in coal-mines (1919);

– Recommendation No. 4 on lead poisoning (Women and Children) (1919);

– Convention No. 13 on White Lead (Painting) (1921);

– Convention No. 28 on Protection against Accidents (Dockers) (1929);

– Recommendation No. 31 on Prevention of Occupational Accidents (1929);

– Convention No. 32 on Protection against Accidents (Dockers, Revised) (1932);

– Convention No. 62 and Recommendation No. 53 on Safety Provisions (Building) (1937);

– Recommendation No. 97 on Protection of Workers' Health (1959);

– Recommendation No. 112 on Occupational Health Services (1959);

- Convention No. 115 and Recommendation No. 114 on Radiation Protection (1960);

- Convention No. 119 and Recommendation No. 118 on the Guarding of Machinery (1963);

- Convention No. 120 and Recommendation No. 120 on Hygiene (Commerce and Offices) (1964);

- Convention No. 127 and Recommendation No. 128 on Maximum Weight (1967);

- Convention No. 134 and Recommendation No. 142 on accident prevention (1970);

- Convention No. 136 and Recommendation No. 144 on Benzene (1971);

- Convention No. 148 and Recommendation No. 156 on the Working Environment (Air Pollution, Noise and Vibration) (1977);

- Convention No. 152 and Recommendation No. 160 on Occupational Safety and Health (Dock Work) (1979);

- Convention No. 155 and Recommendation No. 164 on Occupational Safety and Health (1981);

- Convention No. 161 and Recommendation No. 171 on occupational health services (1985);

- Convention No. 162 and Recommendation No. 172 on asbestos (1986);

- Convention No. 163 and Recommendation No. 173 on seafarers' welfare (1987);

- Convention No. 167 and Recommendation No. 175 on safety and health in construction (1988);

- Convention No. 170 and Recommendation No. 177 on chemicals (1990);

- Convention No. 174 and Recommendation No. 181 on prevention of major industrial accidents (1993);

- Convention No. 176 and Recommendation No. 183 on safety and health in mines (1995).

5. *Labour Inspection*

– Convention No. 81 and Recommendation No. 81 on Labour Inspection (1947);

– Recommendation No. 82 on Labour Inspection (Mines and Transport) (1947);

– Convention No. 129 and Recommendation No. 133 on Labour Inspection (Agriculture) (1969);

– Convention No. 178 and Recommendation No. 185 on Labour Inspection (1996).

6. *Remuneration*

– Convention No. 26 on Minimum Wage-Fixing Machinery (1928);

– Convention No. 95 and Recommendation No. 85 on the Protection of Wages (1949);

– Convention No. 99 on minimum Wage Fixing Machinery (Agriculture) (1951);

– Convention No. 100 and Recommendation No. 90 on Equal Remuneration (1951);

– Convention No. 131 and Recommendation No. 135 on Minimum Wage Fixing (1970);

– Convention No. 158 and Recommendation No. 166 on termination of employment (1982);

– Convention No. 173 and Recommendation No. 180 on the protection of workers' claims (employer's insolvency) (1992).

II. European Norms

A. *Council of Europe instruments*

1. *Treaties*

European Social Charter (1961), Additional Protocol (1988) and revised European Social Charter (1996). See Appendices I and IV above.

2.   *Texts of the Committee of Ministers*

–   Resolution AP(68)1 (also published under the reference Resolution (68)19) on the protection of workers against falls from heights during construction work;

–   Resolution AP(69)6 on safety regulations for electrically-driven and rigidly guided lifts on building sites;

–   Resolution AP(69)7 on safety of workers in the use of certain tannery machinery and equipment;

–   Resolution AP(70)36 on occupational safety of migrant workers;

–   Resolution AP(72)5 on the harmonisation of measures to protect the health of workers in places of employment;

–   Resolution (76)1 on safety services in firms;

–   Resolution AP(80)1 on different means to be applied to prevent the dispersion, reduce concentration in the air and avoid the inhalation of dust at work-places;

–   Resolution AP(81)5 on technical and personal protective measures for the prevention of exposure of workers to asbestos dust.

3.   *Texts of the Parliamentary Assembly*

–   Recommendation 504 (1967) and Resolution 356 (1967) on the political, social and civil situation of women in Europe;

–   Recommendation 730 (1974) and Resolution 565 (1974) on the humanisation of working conditions in the industrial society;

–   Recommendation 919 (1981) on the protection of workers in the case of the insolvency of their employer;

–   Recommendation 1051 on labour market flexibility in a changing economy;

–   Resolution 1056 (1995) on the social policies and stability in the countries of central and eastern Europe;

–   Recommendation 1304 (1996) on the future of social policy;

- Resolution 1101 (1996) on the World trade Organisation and the implementation of the Uruguay Round agreements;

- Recommendation 1308 (1996) on the World Trade Organisation and social rights;

- Recommendation 1324 (1997) on the Parliamentary Assembly contribution to the Second Summit of Heads of State and Government of the Council of Europe;

- Recommendation 1369 on the dangers of asbestos for workers and the environment (1998).

B. *European Union norms*

1. *The Treaty establishing the European Community*

- Article 137 (former Article 118) of the Treaty (revised version):

Paragraph 1 provides that the Council may adopt, by means of directives, in accordance with the procedure referred to in Article 251[1] and after consulting the Economic and Social Committee and the Committee of the Regions, minimum requirements relating in particular to the improvement of health and safety in the working environment and working conditions;

Paragraph 3 provides that the Council may adopt measures unanimously on a proposal from the Commission, after consulting the European Parliament, in particular relating to the protection of workers when their employment contract is terminated and to the conditions of employment for third-country nationals;

- Article 140 (former Article 118 C) of the Treaty (revised version) provides that the Commission shall encourage co-operation between the member states and facilitate the co-ordination of their action, *inter alia*, in relation to the right to

---

[1] By a qualified majority in co-operation with the European Parliament.

work and working conditions and to the prevention of occupational accidents and diseases;

– Article 141 (former Article 119) of the Treaty (revised version) provides that each member state shall ensure that the principle of equal pay for male and female workers is applied and that the Council, in accordance with the procedure referred to in Article 251 and after consulting the Economic and Social Committee, shall adopt measures to ensure the application of the principle of equal opportunities and equal treatment of men and women in matters of employment, including the principle of equal pay for work of equal value;

– Article 142 (former Article 119 A) provides that member states shall endeavour to maintain the existing equivalence between paid holiday schemes.

2.   *Directives*

• Working hours and employment relationships

– Directive 91/533 on an employer's obligation to inform employees of the conditions applicable to the contract or employment relationship;

– Directive 93/104 concerning certain aspects of the organisation of working time;

– Directive 97/81 concerning the Framework Agreement on part-time work concluded by UNICE, CEEP and the ETUC as amended by Directive 98/23.

• Safety and health at work

– Directive 77/576 on the approximation of the laws, regulations and administrative provisions of the member states relating to the provision of safety signs at places of work as amended by Directive 79/640;

– Directive 78/610 on the approximation of the laws, regulations and administrative provisions of the member states on the protection of the health of workers exposed to vinyl chloride monomer;

– Directive 80/1107 on the protection of workers from the risks related to exposure to chemical, physical and biological agents at work as amended by Directive 88/642;

– Directive 82/605 on the protection of workers from the risks related to exposure to metallic lead and its ionic compounds at work (first individual Directive within the meaning of Article 8 of Directive 80/1107);

– Directive 83/477 on the protection of workers from the risks related to exposure to metallic lead and its ionic compounds at work as amended by Directives 91/382 and 98/24 (second individual Directive within the meaning of Article 8 of Directive 80/1107);

– Directive 86/188 on the protection of workers from the risks related to exposure to noise at work as amended by Directive 98/24;

– Directive 88/364 on the protection of workers by the banning of certain specified agents and/or certain work activities (fourth individual Directive within the meaning of Article 8 of Directive 80/1107);

– Directive 89/391 on the introduction of measures to encourage improvements in the safety and health of workers at work;

– Directive 89/654 concerning the minimum safety and health requirements for the workplace (first individual Directive within the meaning of Directive 89/391);

– Directive 89/655 concerning the minimum safety and health requirements for the use of work equipment by workers at work as amended by Directive 95/63 (second individual Directive within the meaning of Directive 89/391);

– Directive 89/656 on the minimum health and safety requirements for the use by workers of personal protective equipment at the workplace as amended by Directive 96/58 (third individual Directive within the meaning of Directive 89/391);

– Directive 90/269 on the minimum health and safety requirements for the for the manual handling of loads where there is a risk particularly of back injury to workers (fourth individual Directive within the meaning of Directive 89/391);

– Directive 90/270 on the minimum health and safety requirements for work with display screen equipment (fifth individual Directive within the meaning of Directive 89/391);

–   Directive 90/394 on the protection of workers from the risks related to exposure to carcinogens at work (sixth individual Directive within the meaning of Directive 89/391);

–   Directive 90/679 on the protection of workers from risks related to exposure to biological agents at work as amended by Directives 93/88, 95/30 and 97/59 (seventh individual Directive within the meaning of Directive 89/391);

–   Directive 91/383 supplementing the measures to encourage improvements in the safety and health at work of workers with a fixed-duration employment relationship or a temporary employment relationship;

–   Directive 92/29 on the minimum safety and health requirements for improved medical treatment on board vessels;

–   Directive 92/57 on the implementation of minimum safety and health requirements at temporary or mobile construction sites (eighth individual Directive within the meaning of Directive 89/391);

–   Directive 92/58 on the minimum requirements for the provision of safety and/or health signs at work (ninth individual Directive within the meaning of Article 16 (1) of Directive 89/391);

–   Directive 92/85 on the introduction of measures to encourage improvements in the safety and health at work of pregnant workers and workers who have recently given birth or are breastfeeding (tenth individual Directive within the meaning of Directive 89/391);

–   Directive 92/91 concerning the minimum requirements for improving the safety and health protection of workers in the mineral-extracting industries through drilling (eleventh individual Directive within the meaning of Directive 89/391);

–   Council Directive 92/104 on the minimum requirements for improving the safety and health protection of workers in surface and underground mineral-extracting industries (twelfth individual Directive within the meaning of Directive 89/391);

–   Directive 93/103 concerning the minimum safety and health requirements for work on board fishing vessels (thirteenth individual Directive within the meaning of Directive 89/391);

— Directive 96/29/Euratom introducing basic norms for the protection of the health of the population and workers against the risks from ionising radiation;

— Directive 96/82 on the control of major-accident hazards involving dangerous substances;

— Directive 98/24 on the protection of the health and safety of workers from the risks related to chemical agents at work (fourteenth individual Directive within the meaning of Directive 89/391).

● Remuneration

— Directive 75/117 on the approximation of the laws of the member states relating to the application of the principle of equal pay for men and women;

— Directive 80/987 on the approximation of the laws of the member states relating to the protection of employees in the event of the insolvency of their employer.

3. *Regulations*

— Regulation No. 2062/94 establishing a European Agency for Safety and Health at Work as amended by Regulation No. 1643/95.

Social Charter monographs

No. 1:   The family

No. 2:   Equality between women and men (new edition)

No. 3:   Children and adolescents

No. 4:   Migrant workers and their families

No. 5:   The right to organise and to bargain collectively

No. 6:   Conditions of employment (new edition)

No. 7:   Social protection (new edition)

No. 8:   Employment, vocational guidance and training

No. 9:   Complaint No.1:1998 : International Commission of Jurists against Portugal

Sales agents for publications of the Council of Europe
Agents de vente des publications du Conseil de l'Europe

Council of Europe Publishing/Editions du Conseil de l'Europe
F-67075 Strasbourg Cedex
Tel.: (33) 03 88 41 25 81 – Fax: (33) 03 88 41 39 10 – E-mail: publishing@coe.int – Web site: http://book.coe.fr